Sketching San Francisco's Neighborhoods

by Eleanor Burke

A visual journey through the well-known and not-so-well-known areas of the city

DEDICATION

For Bernie, my most loyal and supportive friend,
and for Molly, George, Mai Ly and Cody,
in whose company I find so much joy.

INTRODUCTION

Like most San Franciscans, I am inordinately proud of my city. I've lived here all my life, in seven different neighborhoods. I shop, visit friends and family, go to restaurants and events and baseball games in about twenty-four others. Naively, I thought that meant I KNEW this city, and I embarked on a project to sketch it, confident that I had little to learn. Luckily, I was wrong.

Depending on whose boundaries you trust, San Francisco has about 135 neighborhoods within its forty-nine square miles. When I got on my trusty motor scooter to explore them, I kept finding corners I never knew existed. I got into conversations with strangers about their neighborhoods. I read articles and books about the city. Over the next year and a half, I found a wealth of delights: Cayuga Park, the Pemberton Steps, the Bayview Opera House, Brooks Park, Nosh's Dirty Popcorn, Hollywood Park, the Bi-Rite Creamery, Edgehill Drive just for starters.

I have many people to thank. My sister Linda spent countless hours collecting information and accompanying me on walks in exotic parts of the city. Elaine, our AT&T park usher, told me about Cayuga Park and Little Hollywood. Grandson George insisted I do a page on Ft. Funston. He and granddaughter Molly boldly attacked the Seward Street slides and let me photograph them doing so. The enthusiasm of daughters Wendy and Leslie and sister Ann kept me focused, Ann's knowledge of color in the back of my head. Brother Fred has been a first rate PR department. Dorothy gave me great background on St. Francis Wood as did Audrey and Mary on Cottage Row. Buffy told me about Bi-Rite and the Free Farmers Market. Son-in-law Charlie gave me some excellent suggestions as did artist and old friend Nancy, mentor extraordinaire. Son Fred got me in touch with Anh, the printer in Saigon, without whom this book woulo never have seen the light of day. Thanks also to City Guides and the San Francisco Museum and Historical Society, who deserve so much credit for telling the city's stories. The fact that there is still a lot of good stuff missing from this volume I hope encourages the reader to do his own exploring and send me ideas for volume 2.

And finally, my gratitude beyond measure to Audrey, Mary, Liz and Leslie, who did the tedious, time-consuming, heroic job of proofreading and editing.

I hope this book encourages others, both residents and tourists, to go beyond the well-traveled paths and get a taste of the remarkable diversity, color and wide-ranging cultures that make San Francisco so special.

Eleanor Burke
egburke@earthlink.net
2nd edition, 2011

THE NEIGHBORHOODS:

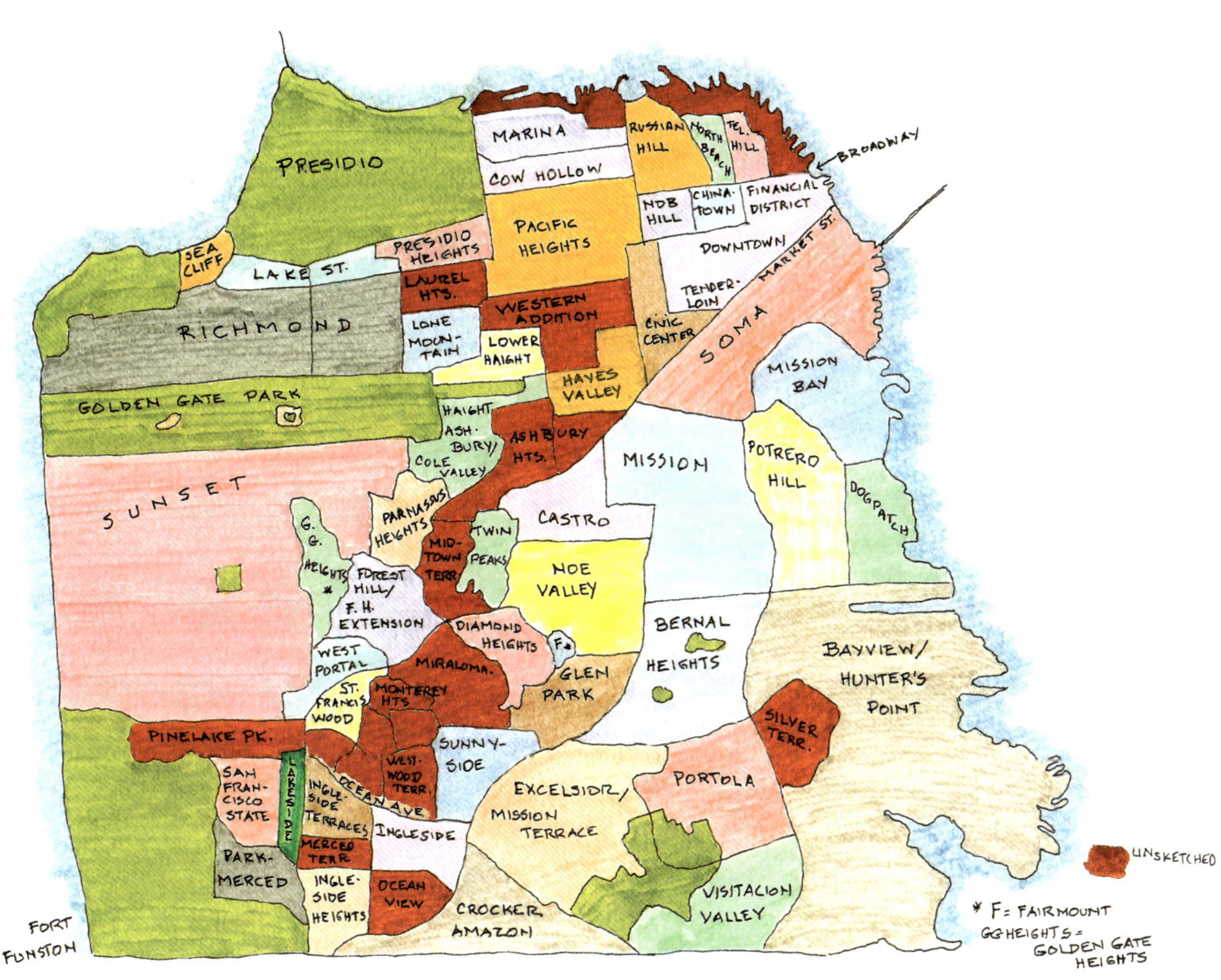

FINANCIAL DISTRICT, EMBARCADERO, UNION SQUARE (DOWNTOWN), TENDERLOIN, SOMA

1. Vaillancourt Fountain
2. Ferry Plaza shops
3. Lotta's Fountain
4. Admission Day Monument
5. Palace Hotel
6. Herbst Building
7. Russ Building
8. 155 Sansome
9. Crocker Galleria
10. Union Square
11. Frank Lloyd Wright building
12. Longshoreman sculpture
13. Rincon Building
14. Audiffred Building
15. Yerba Buena Gardens
16. Contemporary Jewish Museum
17. MOMA
18. Old Mint
19. Chronicle Building
20. 9th Circuit Court
21. AT&T Park
22. South Park
23. Mission Bay
24. Dottie's True Blue Cafe
25. Glide Memorial Church

view from the bay: Embarcadero to Telegraph Hill

THE VAILLANCOURT FOUNTAIN on Justin Herman Plaza is a wonderful place to walk under and around the "waterfalls" and enjoy lunch on the Plaza on a nice day.

Behind is the FERRY BUILDING, where commuter boats dock and visitors from across the bay join locals to shop at the high-end stores for food, kitchen goods, books, wine, mushrooms and more. On Saturdays the Farmers Market is a huge draw.

FERRY PLAZA SHOPS
AND RESTAURANTS

DOWNTOWN ARCHITECTURE

looking west on Market Street toward Twin Peaks with a view of the Hobart Building

looking down Sutter Street toward Market

DOWNTOWN MONUMENTS

Lotta Crabtree was an actress who, as a child in 1853, moved to Grass Valley, CA. There she met Lola Montez, who encouraged her enthusiasms. She came to San Francisco and by 1859 was known as "Miss Lotta, the San Francisco Favorite." Her mother collected all her earnings in gold, which she stored in a steamer trunk. When, eventually, it became overfilled with coins, she invested in real estate, race horses and bonds, and the estate grew substantially. She and her daughter also built fountains, the most famous of which is this one where, every April 18, ceremonies are held to commemorate the '06 earthquake and fire.

THE PALACE HOTEL

Located on the corner of Market and New Montgomery is this elegant treasure of a hotel. The original was opened in 1875 and flourished in the city's champagne and bonanza days. Completely destroyed in the '06 fire, it was rebuilt and renovated more than once, the final one finishing in late 2009.

Look at Maxfield Parish's painting of the Pied Piper of Hamlin in the bar and try counting how many people are in it.

The famous Garden Court with its Austrian crystal chandeliers, Italian marble columns and potted palms set under a huge glass dome is an official city landmark and still, after all these years, a gracious place to meet and eat or take afternoon tea.

Some famous guests of the hotel include President Warren Harding, who died here in 1923; David Kalakaua, the last king of Hawaii; and Dom Pedro, Emperor of Brazil.

SOME DOWNTOWN ICONS

The baroque decoration above is from the Herbst Building on 3rd and Market. Built in 1909 and then remodeled in 1937 by Julia Morgan, it used to be the main office of *The San Francisco Examiner.*

The City Club at 155 Sansome, a 1930 art deco building, has a large Diego Rivera mural inside.

The neo-gothic Russ Building on the right, completed in 1927, is on Montgomery between Pine and Bush. A California State Historical Landmark, it was modeled after Chicago's Tribune Tower and named after Emmanuel Russ, who bought the land it sits on in 1847 for $75.

THE CROCKER GALLERIA

The construction of the Crocker Galleria involved opening up public garden space on the rooftop of the adjoining building, a place where people can relax during lunch or after a grueling day of shopping.

DOWNTOWN

Union Square is the heart of the city's most elegant shopping.

This Frank Lloyd Wright-designed building on Maiden Lane is now an art gallery.

MISSION & STEUART STREETS

The Audiffred Building below right was one of two waterfront buildings to survive the '06 fire. The story is that a saloon keeper offered the crew that was about to dynamite it to make a fire-break a hose cart full of wine and two quarts of whiskey each to spare the building. It worked.

The building was constructed in 1889. The bottom floor was a bar, the second a restaurant, and the top floor was reserved for "leisure activities."

The sculpture left is called "An Injury to One" and is a memorial to two longshoremen killed on Bloody Thursday in 1934, shot while striking against maritime employers.

Below left is the Rincon Center, built in 1940. Inside are twenty-seven murals painted by Diego Rivera-inspired Anton Refregier between 1941-1948. They depict the history of California.

Because he used a lot of red paint - a boy is reading a red book, the father is wearing a red tie, for instance - critics insisted they were communist propaganda, a left wing plot. The furor culminated in a 1953 debate on Capitol Hill. Eventually cooler heads prevailed and the murals were saved.

MISSION STREET

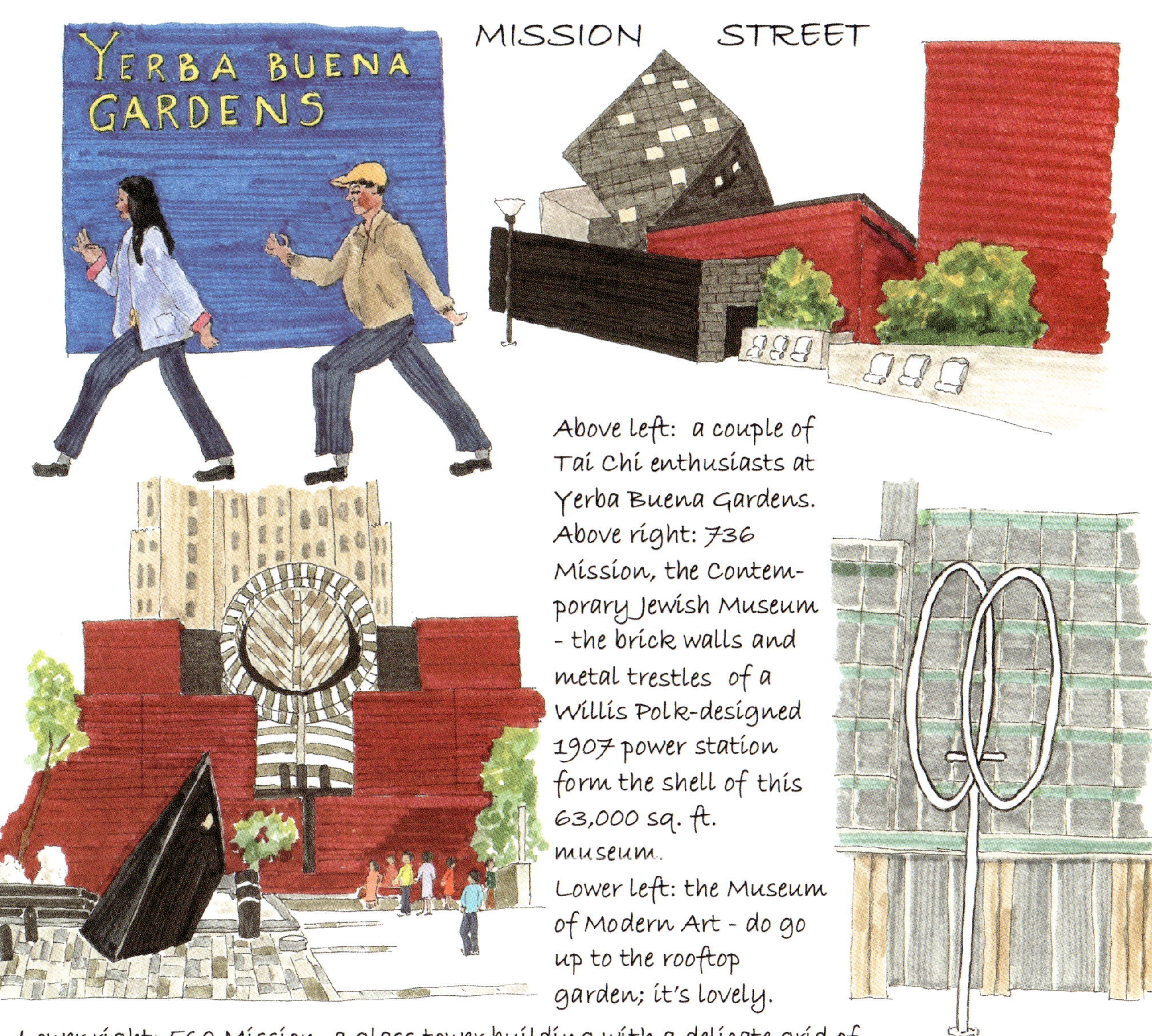

Above left: a couple of Tai Chi enthusiasts at Yerba Buena Gardens.
Above right: 736 Mission, the Contemporary Jewish Museum - the brick walls and metal trestles of a Willis Polk-designed 1907 power station form the shell of this 63,000 sq. ft. museum.
Lower left: the Museum of Modern Art - do go up to the rooftop garden; it's lovely.

Lower right: 560 Mission, a glass tower building with a delicate grid of forest green etched across the clear skin, creating the effect of a Japanese lantern. The sculpture in front is actually two independently moving circles.

PUBLIC ART ALONG THE EMBARCADERO

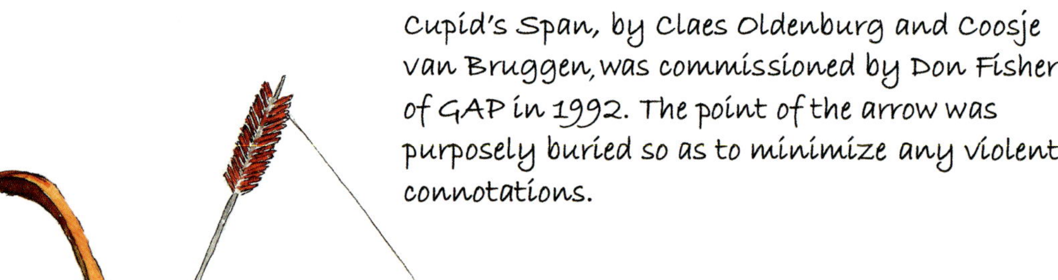

Cupid's Span, by Claes Oldenburg and Coosje van Bruggen, was commissioned by Don Fisher of GAP in 1992. The point of the arrow was purposely buried so as to minimize any violent connotations.

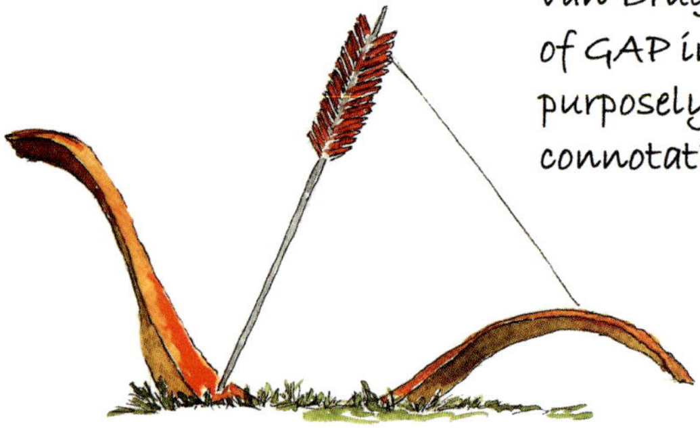

The sculpture below left is on Mission off 2nd Street.

On the right is a fountain by Ruth Asawa on Embarcadero and Howard.

The "Old Mint," actually the second mint in San Francisco, started minting gold coins in 1874. It was closed in 1994, though a current plan would turn it into a museum. The twenty steep stone steps in front lead to a columned portico high above 5th Street.

5th and MISSION:

7th and MISSION:

Right: The beaux arts Ninth Circuit Court, built in 1905, serves the nine Western states. It suffered severe damage in the '89 quake. Subsequent repair cost $91 million.

Above: damage to the Old Mint in the '89 quake.

The San Francisco Chronicle Building, a landmark at 5th and Mission

HIGH-RISE VS. LOW-RISE

An ongoing struggle in this city is the tension between maximizing land values by building up and preserving what is historic. Here is an example: The Infinity on the right at 300 Spear Street, a 35-story look-at-me high-rise, and the low-rise relic of the '06 fire below right, not far away, that is in danger of demolition.

SOUTH PARK: This oval-shaped green, nestled between 2nd and 3rd Streets and Bryant and Brannan, dates back to 1852 and is modeled after one of London's townhouse-ringed squares.

South Park had the first paved streets and sidewalks in the city and was quite the place to live. It began to lose that exclusivity, though, with the construction of the 2nd Street slot, which made

the area more accessible to less affluent citizens. And then when the cable car was built, enabling the wealthy residents to move up to Nob Hill, the neighborhood went into a severe decline that it only recently seems to be coming out of as artists and techies have moved in.

BASEBALL IN SAN FRANCISCO: THE GIANTS

The GIANTS' ball park is THE place to be on game days. Tim Lincecum, two time Cy Young winner, the dogs of the Dog Days of Summer, a Great Blue Heron passing by the yacht harbor next door, McCovey Cove and the pennant flags (left) that show the current standings in the National League West are but a few of the highlights.

AT&T Ball Park is on 3rd and King Streets, with easy access to MUNI, CalTrain and ferries from Marin and the East Bay. Do stop at the Willie Mays statue in front before the game to get infected with Giants fever. If you can't get to a game, then take a ball park tour.

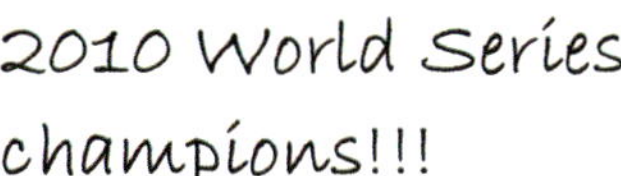

2010 World Series champions!!!

MISSION BAY: a work in progress

The area south of the ball park is being developed into a community that will include the University of California San Francisco's newest campus, condos, shopping and house-boats. The freeway and Twin Peaks are off to the west.

THE TENDERLOIN has always been a tough part of town, so in the early days police were paid extra for working there and thus could afford a more expensive cut of meat, the tenderloin. GLIDE MEMORIAL METHODIST CHURCH, opened in 1929, has been a leading advocate for the homeless and poor.

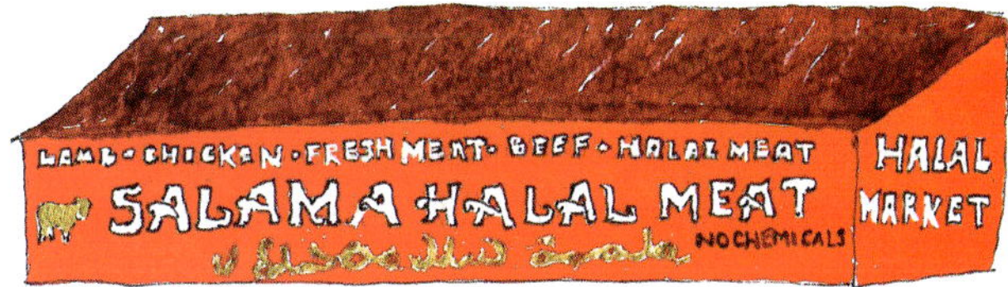

Glide serves three meals a day to the needy, over 750,000 meals a year. It also provides HIV testing, primary health care, crisis intervention, computer training and lots more.

SALAMA HALAL MEAT is an Arab butcher shop on Geary off Leavenworth that sells fresh meat, including whole lambs. Lines are long on Fridays.

DOTTIE'S TRUE BLUE CAFE has to be one of the most successful eateries in the city. Located at 522 Jones, the line is ALWAYS long. It is known for its three-egg omelets, its fat slices of French toast and its homemade breads.

SOUTHEASTERN NEIGHBORHOODS

1. Hells Angels headquarters
2. Esprit Park
3. Pelton cottages
4. 22nd St. commercial, oldest house in Dogpatch
5. Anchor Steam Brewery
6. St. Gregory's Church
7. Vermont Street
8. community garden
9. Potrero Hill Rec. Ctr.
10. 3rd St. commercial
11. Bayview Opera House and gym
12. Portola District entrance
13. view from Mansell St.
14. Visitaction Valley - Leland Avenue
15. Vis. Valley housing
16. Little Holly-wood
17. Cow Palace
18. Excelsior commercial
19. Cayuga Park
20. Crocker-Amazon house
21. Bayview housing

BAYVIEW

Bayview stretches along 3rd Street south of Evans Avenue, west of Hunter's Point. 60% of the neighborhood is African-American, the highest percentage of any neighborhood in San Francisco. It also has the highest rate of home ownership in the city.

THE BAYVIEW OPERA HOUSE

This building dates back to 1888 and was the city's first opera house. In truth it never saw an actual opera performance, but it was a popular site for dramas and vaudeville acts. One actor, David Belasco, later became famous in New York. Pawnee Bill's Medicine Show and some old-time minstrels also played in this 300-seat theater/auditorium. It is now a focal point for local culture and art in the Bayview/Hunter's Point community and provides accessible, diverse, high quality arts education, cultural programs and community events in a safe environment.

The building next door on Newcomb and Mendell is a gym, meticulously restored, with a mural of African-American heroes.

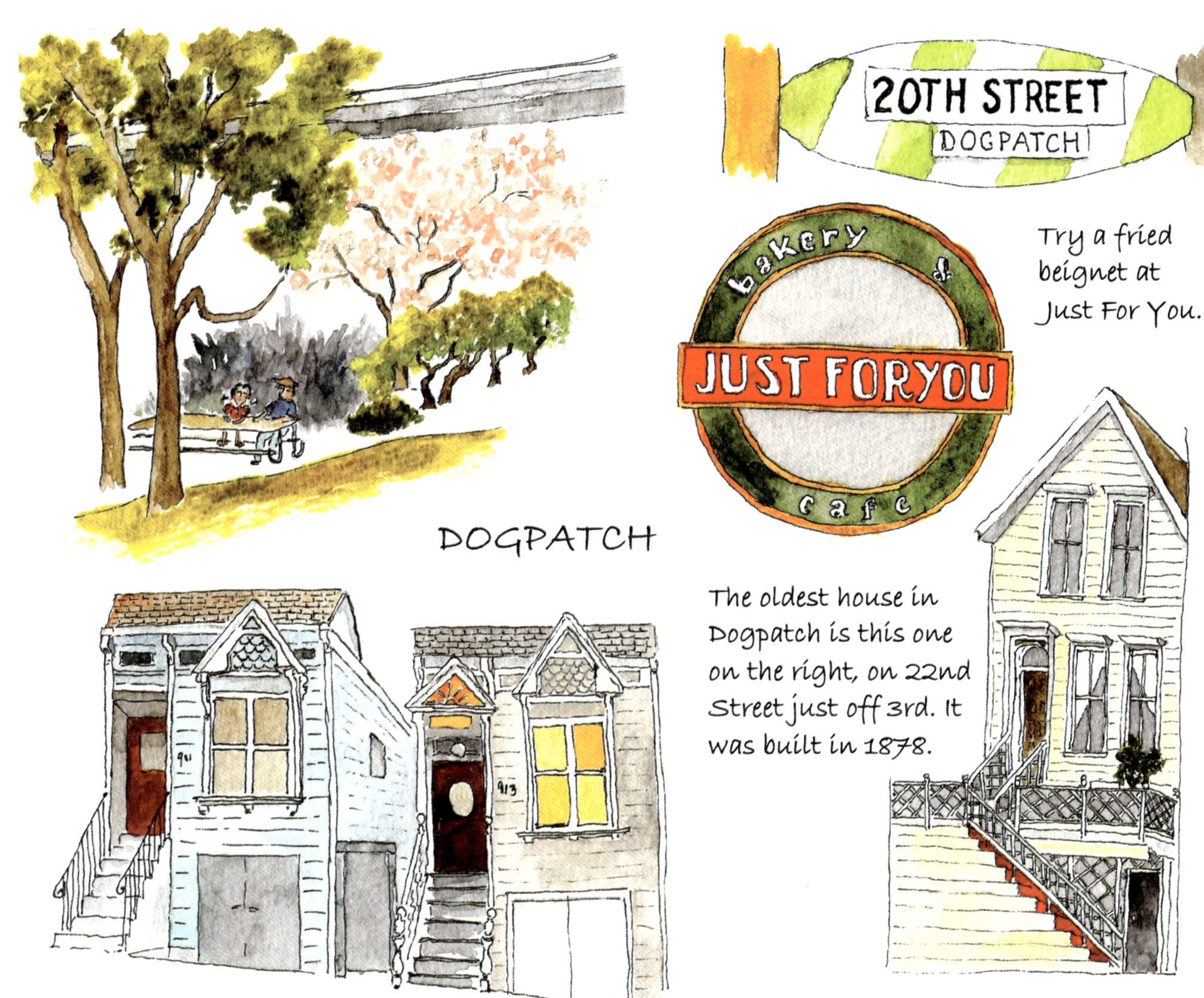

Try a fried beignet at Just For You.

DOGPATCH

The oldest house in Dogpatch is this one on the right, on 22nd Street just off 3rd. It was built in 1878.

DOGPATCH is one of eleven historic districts in the city. It is a neighborhood where warehouses mingle with Victorians and, increasingly, appealing eateries, shops, condos and the remarkable Esprit Park, the local jewel created by Susie Tomkins. The Pelton Cottages above left were built in 1885, when they sold for $854.25.

The name DOGPATCH may have something to do with the dogs that used to run around, trying to catch the source of the smells coming from Butcher Town down the street. Or maybe it came from *Li'l Abner*, who lived in the "uncertain hamlet of Dogpatch." No one seems to know for sure.

The Hells Angels have a place to call their own on Tennessee Street just off 22nd. I'm told they like to be private, though, and don't welcome people ringing their doorbell.

POTRERO HILL

This neighborhood came about as a result of an 1835 land grant to Don Francisco de Haro to graze cattle at "potrero nuevo" (new pasture). Gold Rush settlers started pushing the herd aside and then many waves of immigration followed: Scots in the 1860s, Irish, Russians, Mexicans and finally African-Americans in the 1940's.

The corner of de Haro and Mariposa is the site of two neighborhood icons: St. Gregory's Episcopal Church above, often called "the church of the dancing saints" (go there and you will know why), and Anchor Steam Brewery, founded in 1896 in the days when almost nothing American was worth drinking. The company went through some rough times after its initial success, however, and faced closure when it was bought by Frederick Maytag in 1965. It moved to its current location in 1979. Recently the Maytag family sold it though Anchor Steam will continue. You can take a 90-minute tour of the place, see how beer gets made and sample the product at the end.

VERMONT STREET below right is steeper and has more twists than the more well-known Lombard Street on Russian Hill. The top of this winding plunge is next to McKinley Park on 20th and Vermont and, of course, goes only one way: down.

The Potrero Hill Community Garden looks west toward the incoming fog and is located across the street from McKinley Park.

The Potrero Hill Rec Center above at 801 Arkansas Street has a fading mural of O.J. Simpson on the outside wall of the gym. O.J. grew up on Potrero Hill.

The entrance to the PORTOLA district is on the corner of Mansell and San Bruno Avenue. The main shopping district, though not the only one, is on San Bruno. There is a new library on Bacon and Goettingen. This is a neighborhood in transition: neighborhood-owned shops are giving way to chains and bigger box stores.

The PORTOLA District (accent on the first syllable) is named after the explorer, Gaspar de Portola. When he got here, he found the original residents: the Ohlone Indians. The first group of non-natives were Jewish immigrants and early on the area evolved into a community populated by nurserymen who grew most of the city's flowers. There is a substantial Maltese community here and a growing Asian one.

Streets in this neighborhood are generally named after universities: there is a Harvard Street, a Cambridge Street, a Bowdoin Street, for example. And the views from the top of the hill as you go up into McLaren Park are impressive: you can even see Mt. Tamalpais far to the north.

VISITACION VALLEY

The mural above is on one side of a taqueria on Leland Avenue. Nosh's Dirty Popcorn is a neighborhood icon.

Nosh's Dirty Popcorn

The Popcorn That Tastes Like a Meal

Made With Love, Distributed By Faith, Consumed With Happiness

Ingredients: Love, popcorn, canola oil, spices

Vegan and Diabetic Friendly

www. NoshsDirtyPopcorn. com

Visitacion

Visitacion Valley is a bit of a forgotten neighborhood in the city, though efforts to bring urban amenities that would include a transit-oriented, mixed use complex on the property of the former Schlage Lock Co. and the railyard are in the works. The project will feature a supermarket, condos and parks. The racial makeup of this area is heavily Vietnamese, African-American and Hispanic.

Here are two of the public housing projects in Visitacion Valley, the one just below left built over forty years ago, its low-rise garden apartments still attractive and lively. The newest public housing in Vis. Valley is below right: brightly-painted units, well-tended. There is an older section of public housing on Sunnydale Avenue which is more problematic.

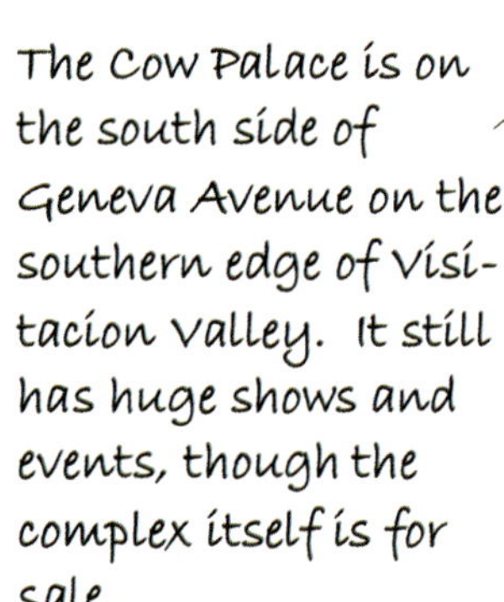

The Cow Palace is on the south side of Geneva Avenue on the southern edge of Visitacion Valley. It still has huge shows and events, though the complex itself is for sale.

LITTLE HOLLYWOOD

The "bird" house is on Lathrop, and the row below is typical of the houses and landscaping of this little village within the city. It also has a lovely park that sits on the hillside on its southern edge.

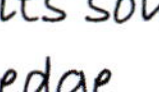

Little Hollywood is one of San Francisco's surprises. Vaguely similar to the well-tended blocks of the Sunset but with much better weather, it is tucked in a triangle off Bayshore, across from Visitacion Valley. Take Blanken Street to enter the neighborhood.

THE EXCELSIOR

Streets in The Excelsior have characteristic names: countries' names going north-south, cities' names going east-west. There used to be a Japan Street and a Germany Street, but those names were changed during World War II and have not been changed back. In earlier days The Excelsior was mostly Italian, Irish and Swiss; today it is one of the most ethnically diverse neighborhoods in the city.

Noteworthy residents have included Jerry Garcia of the Grateful Dead; Joe Cronin, shortstop for the Boston Red Sox and Hall of Famer; and Dan White, the infamous Supervisor who murdered Geroge Moscone and Harvey Milk in 1978.

The mural above, a visual summary of this neighborhood, is on the side of a bakery on Santa Rosa off Mission.

CAYUGA PARK

Don't be put off by the BART trains passing overhead: they add a Disney-land flavor to the place.

This is no ordinary park. Instead it is eleven acres of whimsy, wit and magic with painted wooden sculptures by gardener Demetrio Braceros that represent peace, hope and non-denominational spirituality. Before becoming a city gardener, Braceros worked as a law clerk for Pillsbury, Madison & Sutro, but decided he didn't like wearing a suit and tie every day. So he became a gardener, got hired by Park and Rec and assigned to Cayuga Park with the charge to "change the atmosphere." That he did.

There are two entrances to the park: one at the end of Cayuga Street in Mission Terrace; the other through a gate on Alemany just past Naglee.

THE CROCKER-AMAZON

The Crocker-Amazon covers the area south of Mission Street and Geneva Avenue and extends all the way to Daly City. It is named after Charles Crocker, whose land holdings made up the area. Like The Excelsior next door, it is racially diverse, but with a much larger Filipino community. The neighborhood has a distinctly suburban feel and is often left off maps of San Francisco.

And yes, that is Mount Tamalpais way in the distance.

THE MISSION, THE CASTRO, EUREKA VALLEY, DIAMOND HEIGHTS, NOE VALLEY, GLEN PARK, BERNAL HEIGHTS

1. Mission Dolores
2. Castro & Market
3. 826 Valencia
4. 24th Street
5. Mission High School
6. Roxie Theater
7. 23rd & Shotwell
8. Mission Pool
9. Harvey Milk Academy
10. Women's Center
11. Balmy Alley
12. 18th & Dolores - Bi-Rite
13. Free Farmers Market
14. Kite Hill
15. Seward Street slides
16. Harry Street stairs
17. Laidley Street
18. Free Tibet house
19. Holly Park
20. Bernal Heights Park
21. Cortland Avenue
22. Glen Park: Chenery & Diamond Streets
23. Turquoise Way
24. St. Aidan's Episcopal Church
25. St. Nicholas Syrian Orthodox Church

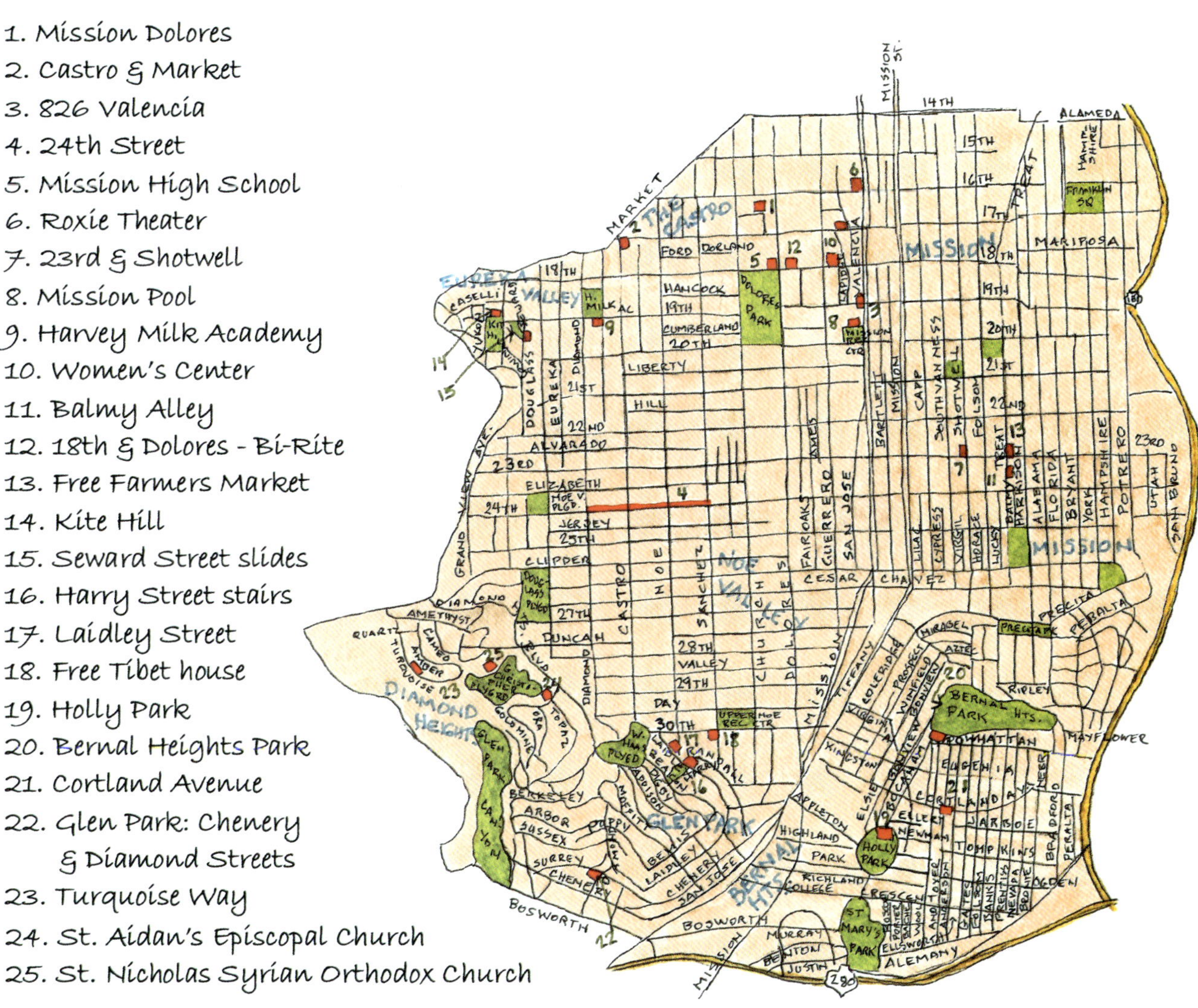

Mission Dolores was built by the local Miwok and Ohlone Indians, whose villages dated back to 500 A.D. The first mass was celebrated just five days before the signing of the Declaration of Independence in 1776. One of twenty-one missions built in California, this one was established by Father Junipero Serra. Its adobe walls are four feet thick.

MISSION DOLORES

Some of the people buried here are known to San Franciscans by street names: William Leidesdorff, an African-American businessman; the Noe family; Lt. Jose Joaquin Moraga; Don Francisco de Haro, the first alcalde (mayor); and Don Luis Arguello, the first governor of Alta California. Also buried here are three victims of vigilantes: James Casey, Charles Cora and "Yankee" Sullivan.

on the right: a Victorian cottage in the neighborhood

THE CASTRO

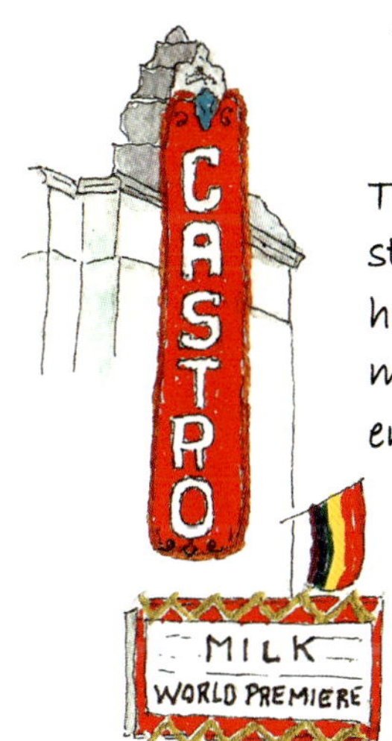

The Castro Theater is a 1930s-style movie house where a real human being plays the mighty Wurlitzer to entertain audiences before a show.

CLIFF'S VARIETY

All American Boy

BILLIARD BOY

The rainbow flag at the intersection of Castro & Market was put up in 1997 to commemorate the twentieth anniversary of the election of Harvey Milk to the Board of Supervisors. Created by Gilbert Baker, it reflects the diversity of the community with its straight, gay, bisexual, lesbian and transgendered population; the number of colors are those of a natural rainbow.

Cliff's Variety is an experience in itself, as are most of the shops on the street, several with suggestive names like "Does your mother know?" and "Hot and Hunky."

826 VALENCIA AND PAXTON GATE

Author Dave Eggers's tongue-in-cheek pirate-theme store is really a mentoring/tutoring center for kids who want help with writing and reading, a model that has been copied in many cities across the country. Paxton Gate next door at 824 Valencia sells plants, candles, garden implements, taxidermy, framed insects and animal skulls.

24th Street is a neighborhood in itself, one of quaint cafes, chic restaurants, craft boutiques, and...my favorite...a mystery book store. Gay and straight families live in this progressive 'hood, where labradors are more common than Republicans.

Built in 1909, the ROXIE on 16th and Valencia is the city's oldest continually operating theater. It offers art and independent films and has recently had a substantial makeover.

man dining with dog

MISSION HIGH SCHOOL is on 18th and Dolores, across from Dolores Park, dubbed Dolores Beach by many of its habitués who enjoy sunbathing there.

BI-RITE CREAMERY and the FREE FARMERS MARKET

Bi-Rite Creamery on 18th off Dolores is one of San Francisco's great treats. Flavors like salted caramel and roasted banana are addictive. But beware: on sunny days the line can be very, very long.

givers

recipients

The Free Farmers Market on 23rd and Treat is held every Sunday afternoon from 12-2, when leftover stuff from the Ferry Plaza Farmers Market is given to anyone who wants it. Bring your own bag.

There are over 500 murals in the Mission District. Below left is one from Balmy Alley, between 24th and 25th Streets and Treat and Harrison, the oldest and most impressive mural alley in the Mission. It started when artists organized protests against military actions in Central America.

The Women's Building on 18th Street between Linda and Lapidge honors women heroes from peace activist Rigoberta Menchu to scientist Marie Curie. The work as a whole is titled Maestropeace.

23rd & Shotwell

a wall of Harvey Milk Academy

Mission Pool

Murals in the Mission can be found almost everywhere: on schools, on commercial establishments, on public pools, on walls of buildings, even on stairways like the one below right.

EUREKA VALLEY

The Seward Street slides, off 20th Street, were built in 1977. Bring a cardboard or a plastic tray to slide on and be prepared to HAVE FUN.

naked ladies

view from Eureka Valley north all the way to Marin County

UPPER NOE VALLEY

The Free Tibet House on 30th and Sanchez

THE FAIRMOUNT

Many of the cottages on Laidley Street have been meticulously redone. They sit on a ledge above Noe Valley.

The Harry Street stairs, which climb from Laidley Street up to Beacon, go from a quaint and colorful street of Victorians and modern architecture through an Amazonian-like jungle to the top, where you have one of the best views in the city.

BERNAL HEIGHTS

a stone stairway in Bernal Heights Park

HOLLY PARK is one of the focal points of this dramatically situated neighborhood. The '06 earthquake put it on the map when refugees came to camp here. In 1907 the people who lived here were carpenters, plumbers, machinists, cigarmakers, plasterers, ship riggers, boilermakers and a shoe cutter. These days it is a popular place for young professionals to buy houses and raise families. Unlike Alamo Square with its gilded Victorians, houses here are modest, a mixture of architectural styles.

Bernal Heights is often referred to as "Maternal Heights" by residents. It is a neighborhood whose families, both gay and straight, all seem to have an abundance of dogs and children.

CORTLAND AVENUE is the main shopping drag for Bernal Heights. Two of its more engaging establishments are Red Hill Books, one of the city's most colorful independent bookstores, and across the street, the Wild Side West, a funky, lively bar.

GLEN PARK

Glen Park is built on the slopes of a natural canyon 500 feet deep, the streets laid out to follow the contours of the steep hillsides. Originally agricultural land like most of the areas outside the downtown area, it had no graded roads until 1922.

In 1928 the Bernal Cut was widened, improving vehicular traffic to this and other southeast San Francisco neighborhoods. But what really opened up Glen Park were the 280 Freeway and BART. Since then property values have soared, though the neighborhood still maintains a village feeling.

some GLEN PARK scenes

DIAMOND HEIGHTS

Diamond Heights was the first project of the San Francisco Planning and Urban Renewal Association (SPUR), intended to use land on the hills in the center of the city and develop it in a way to accommodate housing and the topography of this hilly neighborhood. We lived there, on Turquoise Way (below left) in the early 1960s, when it was a new neighborhood. Now it is a much more mature one with trees on the streets and landscaped gardens as well as a busy shopping center.

DIAMOND HEIGHTS CHURCHES

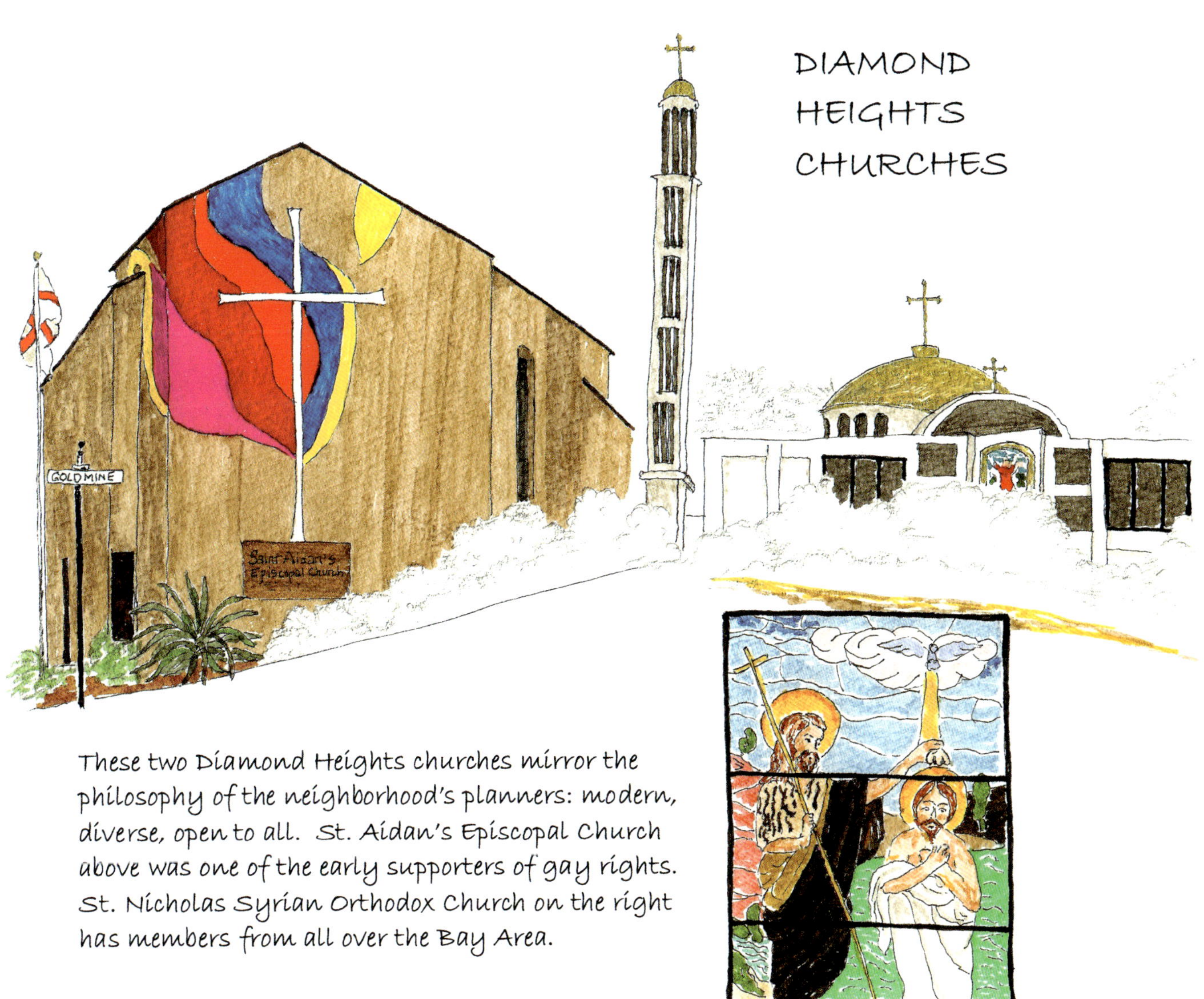

These two Diamond Heights churches mirror the philosophy of the neighborhood's planners: modern, diverse, open to all. St. Aidan's Episcopal Church above was one of the early supporters of gay rights. St. Nicholas Syrian Orthodox Church on the right has members from all over the Bay Area.

WEST OF TWIN PEAKS

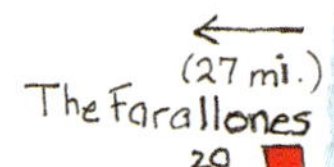

1. St. Francis Wood
2. Forest Hill Clubhouse and steps
3. West Portal Avenue
4. Edgehill Drive
5. Ingleside racetrack and sundial
6. Ocean Ave. library
7. Ocean Ave. shops
8. Sunnyside conservatory
9. Staples Avenue
10. Brooks Park
11. San Francisco State University
12. Parkmerced
13. Lakeside
14. Ft. Funston
15. Sunset row houses
16. Sunset stairs
17. Trocadero
18. Charlie Sava Pool
19. 44th and Judah shopping and eating
20. the Farallones

FOREST HILL

The Forest Hill Clubhouse on Magellan Avenue was designed by Bernard Maybeck in 1919 to look like an English country house.

WEST PORTAL

The Cine Arts Theater on West Portal Avenue is a local destination spot for indie and other high quality films.

West Portal Avenue on a foggy day

FOREST HILL

on a foggy day

Construction on this hilly and affluent neighborhood, though not with the mansion feel of St. Francis Wood, began in 1912 on land originally owned by Adolph Sutro, just as St. Francis Wood was. Homes here are tasteful and large, and it is one of the only non-condominium developments in the city that has an active Homeowners Association, requiring paid membership from all property owners.

looking south

This is also one of the least densely populated neighborhoods in San Francisco.

Magellan Avenue's elms make it one of the few streets in the city with a true tree canopy.

looking north

EDGEHILL DRIVE and SHANGRI-LA

With its whimsical carvings and statues, Edgehill Drive and its sidekick, Shangri-La, may be the most unique streets in San Francisco. It takes a bit of persistence - or luck - to find it. Go up Garcia in Forest Hill Extension and you will get there.

ST. FRANCIS WOOD

St. Francis Circle

This neighborhood of 550 private homes on large lots covers 127 acres and is probably the only area in the city with more green than cement. Dignified gardens that are expensive to maintain show off stately homes block after block. There are also ten acres of parks in this enclave. St. Francis Wood was part of a 725-acre tract sold by Adolph Sutro's children. When the Twin Peaks Tunnel was completed in 1927, St. Francis Wood became an attractive alternative to urban life, a virtual suburban forested community. The developer, Duncan McDuffie, broke the popular San Francisco tradition of 25-foot lots and shoulder-to-shoulder houses. He hired the firm of Frederick Olmsted, which had done Central Park in New York, to plan and landscape this new neighborhood with the goal of retaining as many of the eucalyptus, Monterey pine and cypress trees as possible.

INGLESIDE

Besides the lovely houses that make this area a sort of everyman's dream home neighborhood, there are two unusual attractions: The Sundial and the Racetrack. The Sundial, a 28-foot marble and concrete structure, was built in 1913 and celebrated the opening of the Twin Peaks Tunnel. Below the Sundial was a reflecting pool with a fountain. Encircling it still is a 34-foot in diameter clock face with Roman numerals. Four huge columns sit on the corners, depicting either the four seasons or the four ages of man.

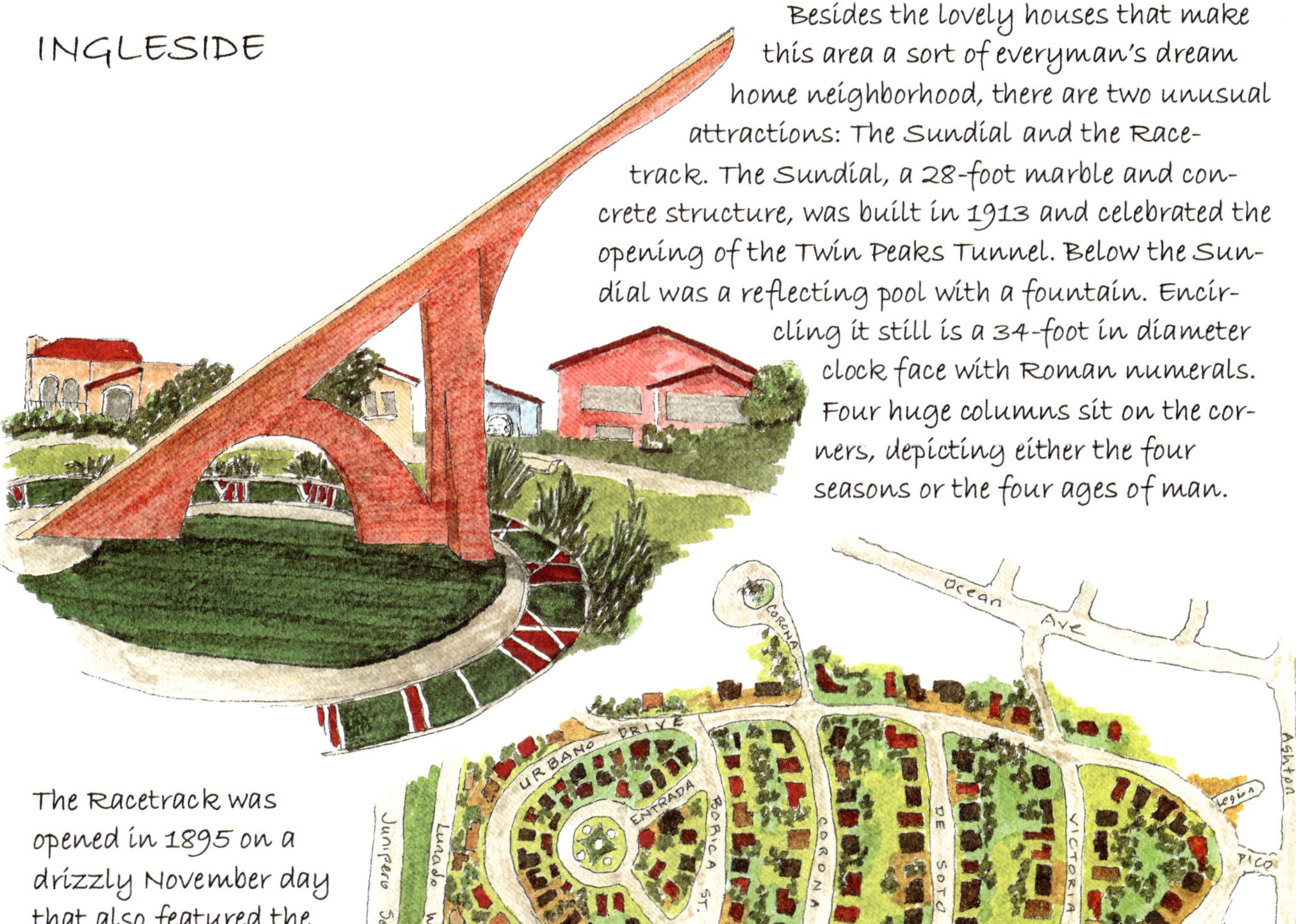

The Racetrack was opened in 1895 on a drizzly November day that also featured the annual Stanford-Cal Big Game on Haight Street, drawing at least 2,000 people away from this event: a horse race at the city's newest tract, a short-lived tradition that ended in 1899 when the SF Board of Supervisors voted that betting on horses and dogs was illegal, a bill that Mayor Phelan signed into law. But it wasn't over: the following year automobile races were held here and the battle for legality went on. The auto races continued until the '06 fire, when the field was used for refugees, never again to be a racetrack of any kind.

INGLESIDE TERRACE

This area was developed in 1913 on 148 acres by Joseph Leonard, developer and designer. Homes are on large lots and in a variety of styles, as these two show: a Mediterranean Revival home and a Craftsman home.

The main local event here is the annual Sundial Park Picnic, at which local residents host bicycle, chariot and wagon races.

Ingleside Terrace was closed to African-Americans until 1957, when Cecil Poole, a Harvard Law School graduate, became its first African-American resident.

Ocean Avenue has several oases. A comfortable coffee shop top above and one of the newest San Francisco library branches at Ocean and Plymouth are especially notable. The city is building/reconstructing twenty-four libraries in neighborhoods around the city as a result of two bond issues voted on in 2000 and 2007. The building above is just one of the results.

INGLESIDE HEIGHTS

sculpture in a driveway on Shields and Arch

BROOKS PARK was established in 1978, seven acres on a hilltop at Shields and Arch, with sweeping views in all directions. It had once been a playground for the Ohlone Indians. Now it includes a community garden and some excellent bird watching opportunities.

SUNNYSIDE

The Sunnyside Conservatory top above, on Monterey between Baden and Congo, was built originally about 1898 by William Merrals, inventor and stargazer, and was restored in 2010. Next to it are two of the whimsical sculptures in the garden.

Staples Avenue is part of a large tract of land developed by the Joost Brothers, who also developed much of Glen Park and other surrounding neighborhoods.

Student Union at San Francisco State University

Lakeside: a neighborhood of tidy houses

PARKMERCED is a development of garden apartments, high-rise apartment buildings and lots of grassy landscaping. The current owners of Parkmerced would like to demolish the charming low-rise units and the open green areas in order to build more high-rise buildings and maximize land values. Ongoing tension here.

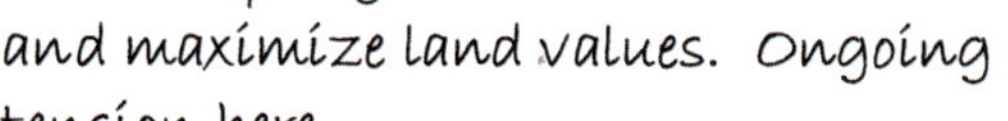

FORT FUNSTON

Fort Funston is all about kite flying and dog walking.

Time for a cookie break, pups.

THE SUNSET

row houses in the Sunset on 35th and 36th Avenues between Kirkham and Lawton

The Farallones, islands which lie twenty-seven miles offshore, are visible on good days from the Sunset District.

SUNSET HEIGHTS

The plaque above left describes how these beautiful mosaic stairs on 16th and Moraga got built: with lots of help from neighbors.

THE CHARLIE SAVA POOL on 19th and Wawona with its excellent facilities is probably the city's prize public pool. Charlie coached ten straight National AAU women's swimming team titles, and Ann Curtis, his greatest swimmer, won thirty-five National Championship gold medals.

THE TROCADERO in Sigmund Stern Grove was built as a hotel in 1892, a rendezvous spot for the elite with cabins around that were rented for the weekend. Several juicy rumors surrounded it: that it was Abe Reuf's hideout when the Reuf-Schmidt machine was smashed after the '06 quake, that it was a speakeasy during Prohibition, and that there are bullet holes in the front door. Later Mrs. Sigmund Stern bought it and deeded it to the city. Nowadays, because of its unusually good natural accoustics, it is the site of weekly summer concerts.

44th and Judah is an up-and-coming neighborhood with colorful stores and a couple of comfortable eateries. The wall on the Outerlands Cafe has a mural of stacked-up plastic bottles. My wonderful motor scooter is parked on the right below.

GOLDEN GATE PARK

1. Dutch Windmill
2. Beach Chalet murals
3. Portals of the Past
4. Japanese Tea Garden
5. DeYoung Museum
6. Academy of Sciences
7. Conservatory of Flowers

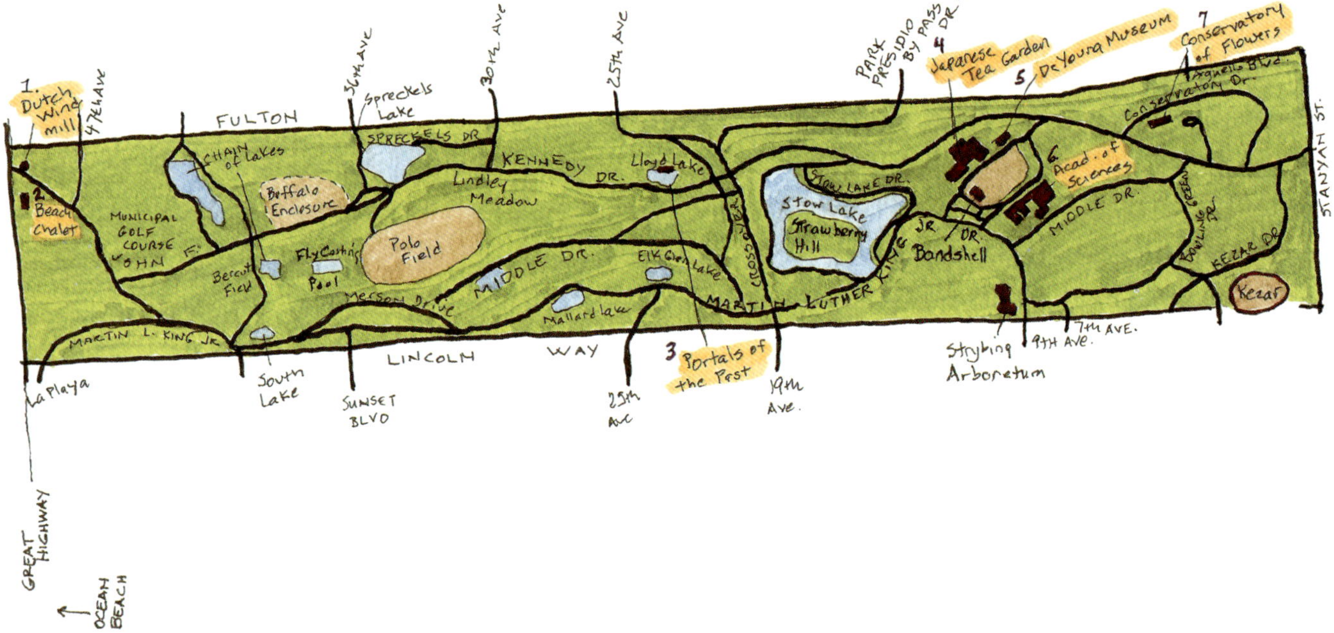

THE CONSERVATORY OF FLOWERS

Restored in 2003 after severe damage from the '89 Loma Prieta quake, this Victorian-style building houses a wide variety of plants and ongoing exhibits that range from butterflies to model trains. It was originally built in 1879, commissioned by millionaire James Lick, who brought it in pieces from England, then let it languish on the grounds of his mansion before finally bequeathing it to the city, a beautiful and graceful gift to San Francisco.

THE DE YOUNG MUSEUM

white poppies growing on the living roof of the Academy of Sciences across the way from the De Young

The De Young first opened in 1895, a by-product of the California Midwinter International Exposition. Damage from the '89 Loma Prieta quake meant a new museum had to be built, and that one opened in 2005, clad in perforated copper plates which change with exposure to the elements. An observation tower on the top floor is open to the public and offers views north to Marin and the Richmond District, south to the Sunset District.

Golden Gate Park, three miles long and half a mile wide, is larger than Central Park in New York. It covers 1,013 acres and includes over a million trees, nine lakes, several fly casting ponds, two major museums, gardens, dells and bike/hiking paths - and more. STOW LAKE, completed in 1893, is an oasis where you can rent a boat and enjoy a quiet and romantic paddle around the large hill/island in the middle.

THE ACADEMY OF SCIENCES is a remarkable experience. Its living roof covers two and a half acres with native plants. Its rain forest, where the temperature is a constant 79 degrees with 79% humidity, has 1,600 live animals. The meandering aquarium has 40,000 aquatic animals. It is the greenest museum in the country and is drawing 80,000 visitors a year. Don't miss the planetarium show.

SOME RESIDENTS OF THE ACADEMY OF SCIENCES

THE JAPANESE TEA GARDEN

The Japanese Tea Garden was also an outgrowth of the 1894 Midwinter Exposition. The Moon Bridge, the tea house and the pond in front of the tea house with the little island in the middle are all part of the original exhibit.

PORTALS OF THE PAST

On the right is a remnant of the '06 quake, all that was left of the 1891 mansion of Alban Towne on the site of the Masonic Building on Nob Hill. It was brought to Golden Gate Park, where it sits on Lloyd Lake, an emblem of loss in the city before rebuilding began.

THE DUTCH WINDMILL

The windmill at the western end of G.G. Park was a gift from Queen Wilhelmina of Holland to the city of SF.

BEACH CHALET MURALS

The frescoes and tile murals of Beach Chalet are on the ground floor of the building and extend all the way up the staircase to a second-floor microbrewery. They were done in 1936 by Lucien Labaudt and restored in 1988.

THE HEART OF SAN FRANCISCO

1. Haight-Ashbury shops
2. Lower Haight shops
3. "new" mint
4. USF - Fromm Institute
5. Edgewood Drive
6. Twin Peaks view
7. Pemberton steps
8. Kezar
9. Cole Valley commercial
10. City Hall
11. Davies Symphony Hall
12. Asian Art Museum
13. Main Library
14. Alamo Square
15. Seven Sisters
16. UCSF (Univ. of California - San Francisco)
17. Japantown
18. Fillmore - the jazz district

THREE ICONS OF HAIGHT STREET:

AMOEBA MUSIC has the best selection of cd's, both new and used, that I have found - and a staff that will drop whatever they're doing to help you. Amazing.

Amoeba Music

HAIGHT ←1500
ASHBURY ←600

The RED VIC is a 16-room B&B. Visitors hang out in the Peace Cafe, where they talk about ways to create a peaceful world.

The HAIGHT-ASHBURY FREE MEDICAL CLINIC performed saintly services during the hippie years, when it treated people strung out on drugs or suffering from HIV. It is still in business, helping people with the same problems.

HAIGHT ASHBURY FREE MEDICAL CLINIC

A walk along Haight Street will prove colorful, quirky and exotic. You will find good food and even a practical item or two.

Pork Store
PorkStore Cafe
PEOPLE'S
CAFE
NAVY
AARDVARK'S
CHEAP THRILLS

THE LOWER HAIGHT

The discovery of gold was responsible for the building of the original mints in SF. The subsequent discovery of silver resuscitated the need for a "new" mint, so this one was built on Herman off Market and opened in 1937, the same year as the Golden Gate Bridge.

DOE, at 629A Haight just west of Steiner, is a miniature department store.

This neighborhood may be more punk than peace, but it has fifteen historical landmarks, including the one above right: probably the oldest residence in the city, built in 1852, New Orleans style. It now sits at 1111 Oak Street. The Lower Haight had 48,000 Victorians before the '06 fire; only 14,000 are still standing.

TWIN PEAKS

With drop-dead views of downtown and the Bay and even Mt. Diablo way over in Contra Costa County, this is a gorgeous neighborhood with an impressive array of beautifully designed houses in styles that range from Mediterranean to modern on streets that follow the contours of Twin Peaks, the second highest hill in the city. Mt. Davidson is the highest.

PARNASSUS HEIGHTS

EDGEWOOD AVENUE

above right: There *are* houses on this brick-paved street, but you wouldn't know it in February, when the plum trees bloom.

the clock tower on Parnassus Avenue

UCSF Medical Center
505 Parnassus Avenue

UC MEDICAL SCHOOL'S huge campus on Parnassus Heights serves many communities; its doctors and research facilities are respected around the world.

THE PEMBERTON STEPS

This walkway from Twin Peaks into the Cole Valley is lovely. I especially like the English style cottage above right with its well-tended garden. Great views - I recommend walking DOWN and not up.

COLE VALLEY

COLE VALLEY, birthplace of Cole Hardware and home of its main store, is the former home of Craig Newmark, founder of Craigslist.

Above right is a selection of natural remedies at a store on Cole Street.

KEZAR (top right) is a former stadium, where the 49ers used to play before Candlestick. It now hosts amateur and recreational sports leagues and high school football games, including the city championship game, known popularly as the Turkey Bowl.

CITY HALL

This beaux arts masterpiece, heavily renovated after nasty damage from the '89 Loma Prieta quake, was originally built in 1915, designed by Arthur Brown, who also designed Coit Tower, the Opera House and Temple Emanu-el. Its dome is the fifth-largest in the world and its marble staircase magnificent.

Some notable events that have taken place here: the marriage of Joe DiMaggio and Marilyn Monroe in 1954, and the tragic murder of Mayor George Moscone and Supervisor Harvey Milk by Supervisor Dan White in 1978.

THE SAN FRANCISCO SYMPHONY

Davies Symphony Hall was constructed in 1980.

Nadya Tichman, concertmaster for this evening, the San Francisco Symphony Chorus and John Relyea, bass baritone, perform *Belshazzar's Feast.*

A symphony orchestra was first formed in San Francisco after the '06 quake and started giving concerts in 1911. Its success since then is mirrored in its numbers: nearly 600,000 people hear over 220 of its concerts and presentations every year, and nearly 60,000 people hear the SF Symphony at no cost each season.
Michael Tilson Thomas, director since 1995, is largely responsible for its success, putting our symphony on the international scene with tours and recordings that widen its recognition as a first-rate orchestra.

THE ASIAN ART MUSEUM

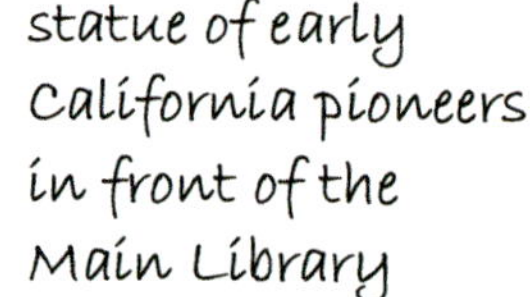

statue of early California pioneers in front of the Main Library

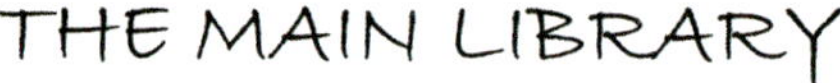

THE MAIN LIBRARY

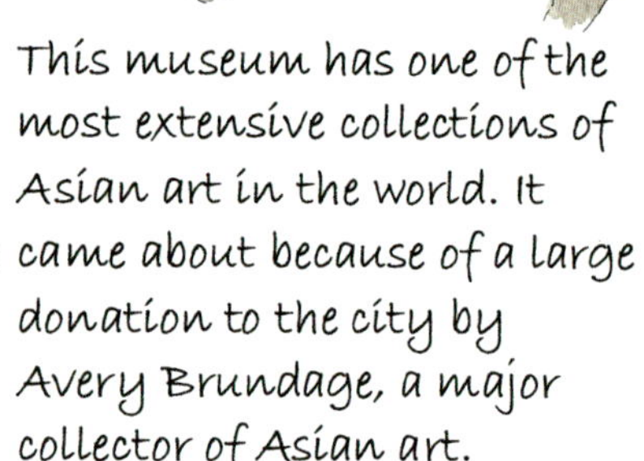

This museum has one of the most extensive collections of Asian art in the world. It came about because of a large donation to the city by Avery Brundage, a major collector of Asian art.

The Main Library opened at its current location at 100 Larkin Street in 1996, an impressive beaux arts building. In addition to its book collection, it is a San Francisco history center and a home of Book Arts and special collections. The interior scene right is a five-story atrium.

HAYES VALLEY is a collection of SoHo type galleries and ultra-chic boutiques, punctuated by trendy eateries and the arts complex which includes the San Francisco Conservatory of Music. Its appeal as a neighborhood was greatly enhanced by the tearing down of the Central Freeway after the '89 Loma Prieta quake. Current freeway access from OCtavia Street with its landscaping and open space has been a boon.

ALAMO SQUARE is probably the only neighborhood in the city that can showcase every kind of Victorian: flat front Italianates, slanted bay Italianates, the more gaudily embellished Stick Eastlakes and finally the true gilded ladies: the Queen Annes.

Most Victorians were built between 1870 and 1890. The Gold Rush was over by then and the Silver Rush was winding down. But San Francisco was growing. Gold miners settled in this neighborhood, which had been a half-way watering stop between the Presidio and Mission Dolores. Then, as San Francisco grew, it spread west and people built on narrow lots in order to accommodate more houses. In 1870 the population of the city was 150,000; by 1900 it had swollen to 342,000. This was the Gilded Age of Victorians, an era of buoyant optimism: the baroque decorations on the houses show that spirit.

The WESTERFIELD HOUSE, right, was built in 1889. It is a gothic style Victorian built for a confectioner, Henry Westerfield. Its top floor has 360-degree views and was featured in Tom Wolfe's *The Electric Kool Aid Acid Test* as home to one of San Francisco's first hippie communities in 1968.

The famous "Seven Sisters" of Alamo Square with the backdrop of downtown San Francisco

WINDOWS OF ALAMO SQUARE

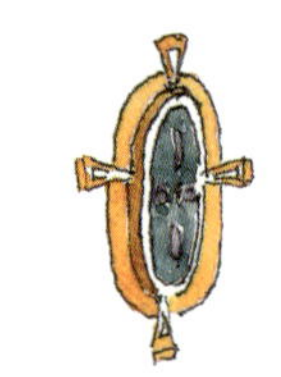

THE FROMM INSTITUTE is college for seniors. It is located at the University of San Francisco and offers non-credit, no assignment (usually) classes for us folks over fifty who have no objective other than to learn. It came about in 1976 with the support of Hanna and Alfred Fromm, refugees from Nazi Germany. Alfred became a wine distributor while Hanna ardently devoted herself to an active intellectual life for retirees.

The Fromm program now enrolls about 1250 students and offers 75 courses in its three-session year with topics covering the humanities, arts and sciences. It has become a model for the Osher Lifelong Learning Institutes that have been established at over 120 colleges and universities all over the country.

JAPANTOWN

Japantown basically extends from Fillmore Street on the west to Gough Street on the east, between Sutter and Geary Streets.

my favorite stationery store in the city: Kinokuniya

Located in the heart of Japantown, the five-tiered Peace Pagoda was erected in 1968 as a symbol of friendship between Japan and the United States.

THE FILLMORE

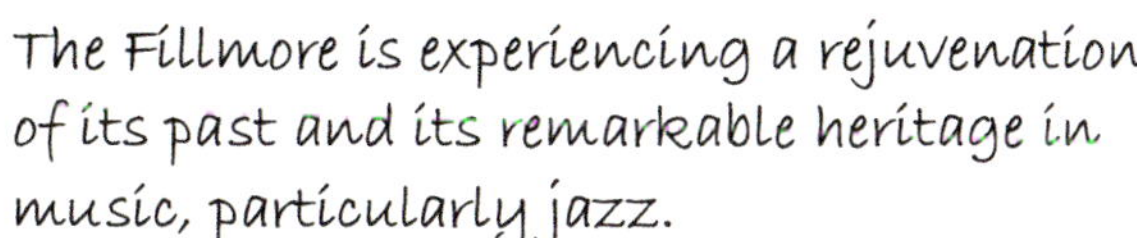

The Fillmore is experiencing a rejuvenation of its past and its remarkable heritage in music, particularly jazz.

NORTHEAST SAN FRANCISCO

1. Grace Cathedral
2. Huntington Park
3. Masonic Auditorium
4. Willis Polk balustrade
5. Marshall houses
6. Octagon house
7. Polk-Williams house
8. Vallejo & Jones Streets
9. Allegro
10. Polk St. commercial
11. Polk Gulch: Swan's, Little Saigon, mural
12. Filbert St. steps
13. City Lights
14. Stinking Rose
15. O'Reilly's
16. Beach Blanket Babylon
17. Molinari's
18. Buena Vista Cafe
19. Aquatic Park
20. South End Rowing Club
21. Coit Tower
22. Fishermans Wharf
23. Ross Alley
24. United Commercial Bank
25. Chinese Hospital
26. Alcatraz

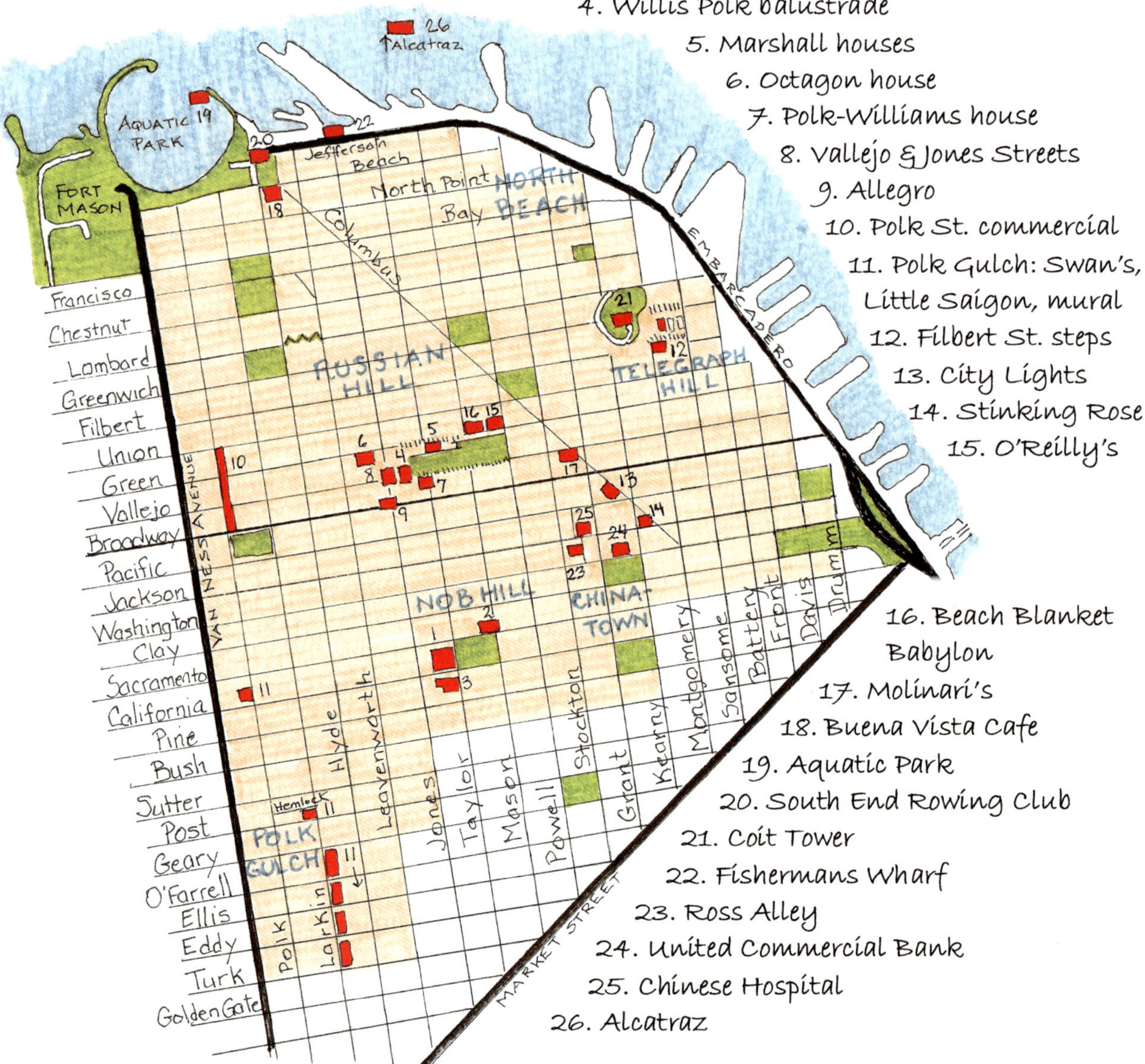

NOB HILL

Some say this is where God stays when he comes to San Francisco. Located on ultra-elegant Nob Hill, Lewis Hobart-designed Grace Cathedral, built after the '06 fire, rises above Huntington Park across the street with great poise. One of its noteworthy features is its Ghiberti doors, one of three copies in the world of the Baptistry door of the Duomo in Florence, Italy. Depicted on these doors are scenes from the Old and New Testaments done in an innovative graded relief. The cathedral also has some magnificent stained glass windows covering subjects that range from Albert Einstein to John Glenn, from Moses to Martin Luther King, Jr. Finally, there are labyrinths both inside and out, medieval meditation exercises to get your mind at ease before attending services.

Charlie Crocker was not popular. He owned most, but not all, of the land in the square block of Jones, Taylor, California and Sacramento. A tiny cottage owned by Nicholas Yung, a German immigrant, sat in his way, and Yung refused to sell. Crocker then put up a forty-foot spite fence, plunging Yung into darkness. It stayed there until both of them died and Crocker's heirs could finally purchase the property, which they then donated for the building of the cathedral.

THE MASONIC AUDITORIUM was built in the 1950s on the site of the Towne Mansion, which burned in '06. Just below is a frieze on its north wall. There are no glass windows in this building; windows are stained Lucite.

HUNTINGTON PARK below left used to be the site of the Colton Mansion. Colton's widow sold it to Collis Huntington, a New York financier, who called it Henry and Arabella Huntinton Park. It was supposed to be only for rich kids and their governesses.

THE PACIFIC UNION CLUB just east of the park was built from silver money by the Flood family and is the only pre-fire mansion on Nob Hill to survive. The Silver Boom from the Comstock Lode produced more wealth than the Gold Rush, but silver is more expensive to extract, so shares were sold to finance the operation of the mines. Two saloon owners, William O'Brien and James Flood, got some profitable tips from tipsy customers, the word on silver being their bonanza.

RUSSIAN HILL

1045 Green, left, was built in 1867, remodeled in 1910. It has both Italianate and Craftsman features.

Russian Hill gets its name from the headstones of several Russian sailors, probably seal hunters, found on the top of the Vallejo Street hill above. The headstones were inscribed in Cyrillic and marked with black Orthodox crosses. Above left are probably the oldest houses on the hill, all much remodeled, especially the large one in the middle that Horatio Livermore built in 1854. The pair behind it, 1034-36 Vallejo, are the MARSHALL HOUSES, designed by amateur architect Rev. Joseph Worcester in 1888 for David Marshall, one of his parishoners at the Swedenborgian Church in Pacific Heights. This simple shingle-style was popular on Russian Hill. The BALUSTRADE at Vallejo and Jones was designed by Willis Polk in 1914. The ramparts on each end provide a formal entrance to the area above, reinforcing the sense of enclave. Polk also designed #1,3,5 and 7 Russian Hill Place, commissioned by Norman Livermore, and 1015-19 Vallejo, the Polk-Williams house at the very top of the hill.

Margot Patterson-Doss once described Russian Hill as a place where "a privileged handful of people eat their cake of urbanity and have rural seclusion too." The top of the hill provides several such oases.

The Polk-Williams house on the right was built in 1892, designed by Willis Polk.

The terraced stairway below on Vallejo and Taylor replaced a goat path and was also designed by Willis Polk.

Below is the Feusier Octagon house at 1067 Green, built in 1857, though its mansard roof and cupola weren't added until the 1880s.

view from Russian Hill toward Telegraph Hill

The cable car, ideally suited to the city's topography, was a tremendous boon to its development. In the 1870s and '80s one could reach hitherto inaccessible parts of the city for five cents a ride. New areas of the city were then open to development, and property values tripled wherever the lines went. By the 1880s, eight different lines extended 112 miles up Telegraph, Nob and Russian Hills, out to the Presidio, to Golden Gate Park and the Cliff House. Then in the 1890s, with the advent of electricity, electric street cars and trolley buses began replacing cable cars. Only three lines remain today.

Ina Coolbrith Park begins on Taylor and Mason with a bench, then plunges down into North Beach below. Ina was a poet.

POLK STREET SHOPS and ALLEGRO

Upper Polk has more than its share of coffee shops and restaurants, but it also has a variety of chic shops, like "Les Cent Culottes" and "Bow Wow Meow."

Allegro on Broadway and Jones hosts a party every election day - for the Democratic ticket, of course.

The former Alhambra Theater, modeled after The Citadel in Spain, is now a gym where you can work on your self-improvement program.

POLK GULCH

a Thai video store

Lower Polk Street as well as lower Larkin Street is often called Little Saigon; if you want a Vietnamese meal or just a take-out sandwich, you can find it there.

The mural below is on Hemlock Alley between Polk and Larkin - reminiscent of the Mission murals but with a distinctive Asian flavor.

SWAN OYSTER DEPOT is THE place to go for fresh seafood, especially Dungeness crab on Christmas Eve, as this group here knows. Or just have a shrimp cocktail at the counter. The Italian family that runs this place is half the fun.

COLUMBUS AVENUE: City Lights below is a landmark to poets and poetry, a monument to freedom of speech. Founded in 1953 by Lawrence Ferlinghetti and Peter Martin as the nation's first all-paperback bookstore, it added City Lights Publishing in 1955 when Ferlinghetti, who had decided to promote the works of Beat poets, became the sole owner.

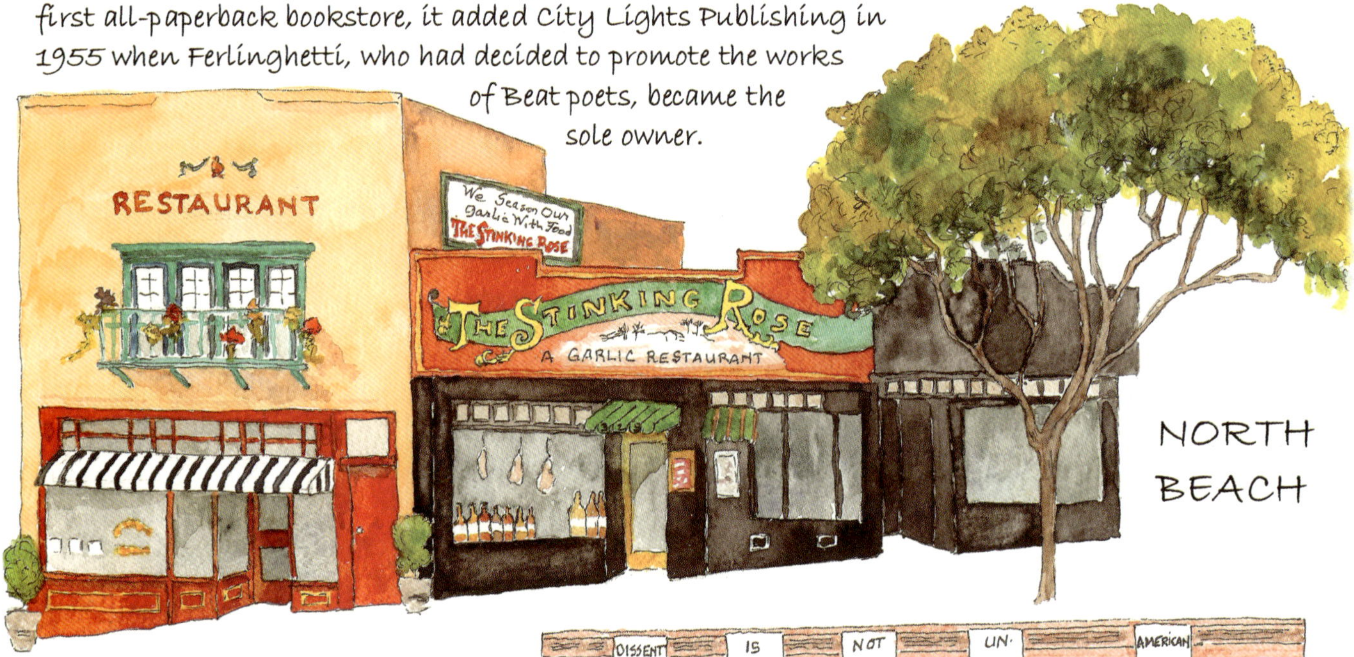

NORTH BEACH

Over the years City Lights has introduced such writers as Allan Ginsberg and Jack Kerouac. In 2001 the store became a local landmark because of its seminal role in the literary and cultural development of San Francisco and the nation and for championing First Amendment rights.

NORTH BEACH SCENES

Molinari's Delicatessan below at 373 Columbus Avenue between Vallejo and Green is a North Beach legend.

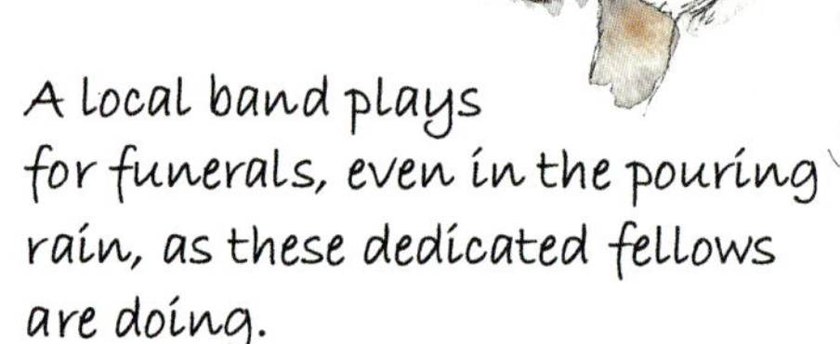

A local band plays for funerals, even in the pouring rain, as these dedicated fellows are doing.

On the right is a mural of James Joyce and Brendan Behan - and Joyce's Irish Setter - at O'Reilly's pub on Green Street off Columbus.

COIT TOWER

Life during the Depression: above, a robbery on Montgomery Street; below, farm laborers in the Valley who have joined the union.

Up the staircase to the second floor you will see depictions of Eleanor Roosevelt (below left) and the Stanford-Cal Big Game.

This iconic tower, mistakenly thought by many to depict a fire hose, was the gift of Lillie Hitchcock Coit in 1933. Lillie greatly admired the city's fire department, which had acted so heroically during the '06 fires. The tower was designed by Arthur Brown. Do take a City Guides tour; you will hear all about these wonderful murals, commissioned as a WPA project during the Great Depression, and it's the only way to see the murals up the stairs.

TELEGRAPH HILL

The WILD PARROTS of Telegraph Hill, a growing flock of conures who squawk boisterously as they make their daily rounds across northern San Francisco, were made famous by Mark Bittner in his book and film about them.

The art moderne MALLOCH APARTMENTS at 1360 Montgomery Street below right are in contrast to the simple wood carpenter's gothic entrance below left on the Filbert Street steps. The apartments were commissioned in 1937 to commemorate the opening of the Bay Bridge, which they overlook. Streamlined chic, the building's facade is cloaked with silver murals that illustrate scenes of Western lore and innovations.

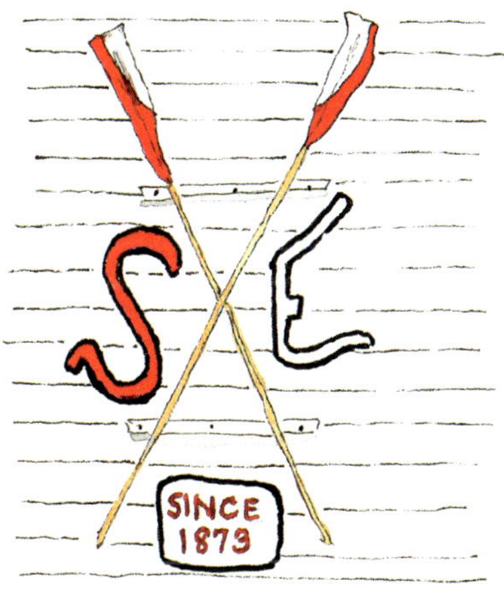

The SOUTH END ROWING CLUB, founded in 1873, is located at 500 Jefferson Street. Activities include rowing, swimming, handball and running.

FISHERMANS WHARF

Fishermans Wharf is the most popular tourist destination in the city. In spite of the distraction of tourists, it remains a working harbor.

ALCATRAZ, no longer a federal prison, once housed notorious felons like Al Capone, Robert Stroud (The Birdman of Alcatraz) and Machine Gun Kelly.

The BALCLUTHA, built in 1886, is part of America's only floating national park and the largest fleet of historical vessels in the world. Others in the fleet include the C.A. Thayer, a sailing lumber schooner; the Eureka, an 1890 ferry boat; the Grace Quan, a junk; and the Alma, a schooner.

THE BUENA VISTA, on Beach and Hyde, has long been a gathering place for those who enjoy Irish coffee on a foggy day - or a sunny one.

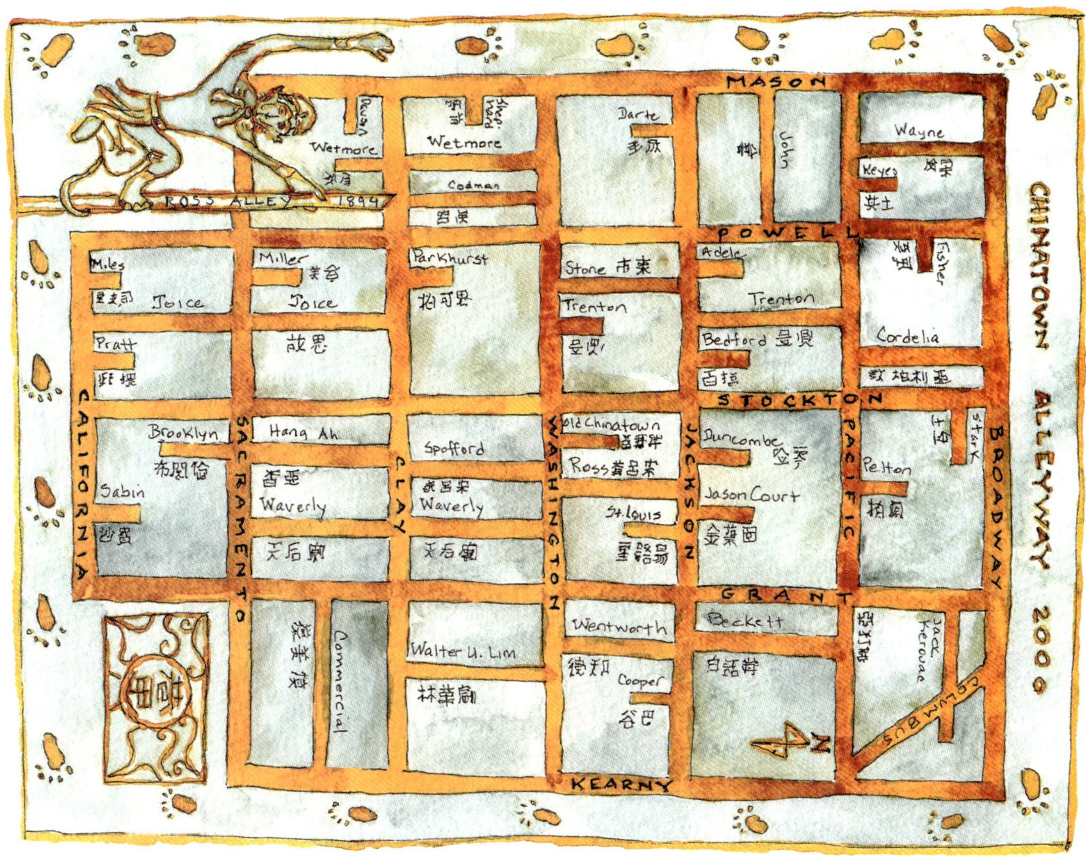

CHINATOWN:

This bilingual map of Chinatown is actually a bronze plaque set into the pavement in Ross Alley.

ROSS ALLEY

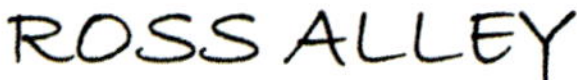

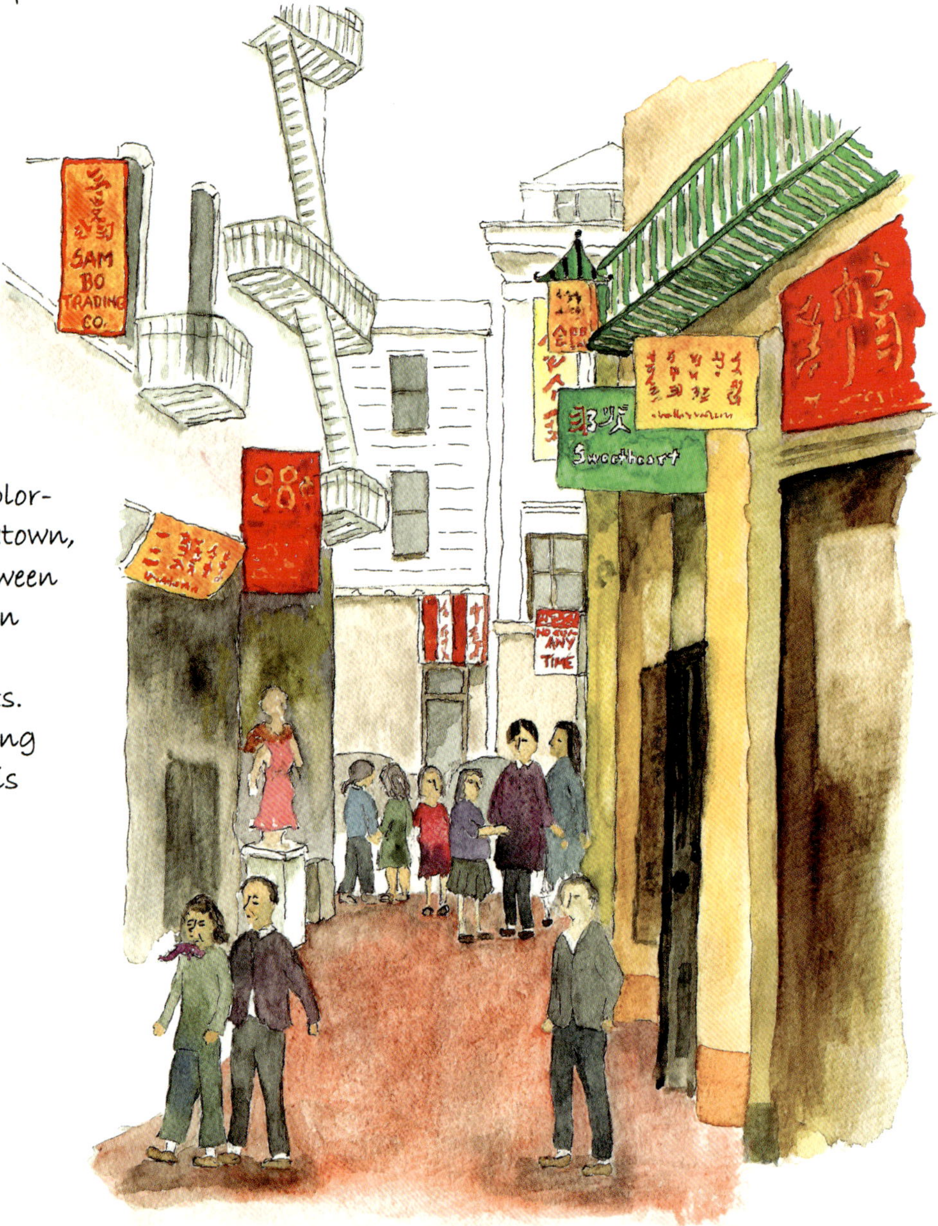

One of the many colorful alleys in Chinatown, Ross Alley sits between Grant and Stockton and Jackson and Washington Streets. An Old World feeling predominates in this neighborhood.

LIFE IN CHINATOWN

playing mah jongg

making fortune cookies

playing cards in Portsmouth Square

reading the newspaper in the Hang Ah Tea Room

There are two Chinatowns: the one on Grant Avenue belongs to the tourists, the other belongs to the locals. These ladies are locals, enjoying a sunny day in a small park on Pacific and Powell Streets.

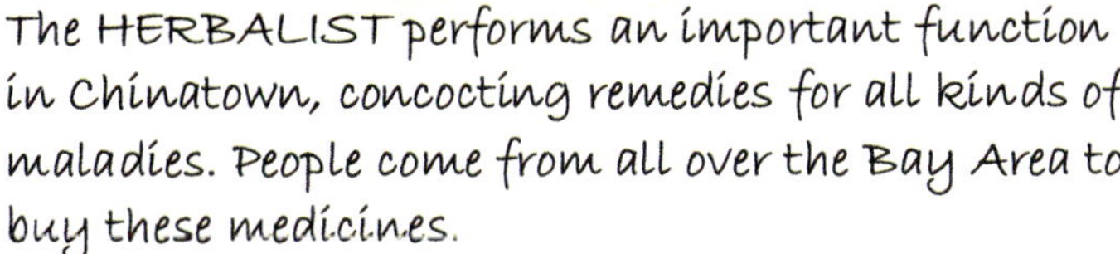

The HERBALIST performs an important function in Chinatown, concocting remedies for all kinds of maladies. People come from all over the Bay Area to buy these medicines.

The East West Bank above right used to be the Chinatown telephone exchange. Every operator could speak five Chinese dialects, and every one of them knew the business of everyone in Chinatown.

Chinatown is San Francisco's second most popular tourist attraction after Fishermans Wharf. A not-so-well-known fact: America has one million surnames for its population of 310 million. China has just 10,000 surnames for its population of 1.3 billion.

CHINESE MEDICINE

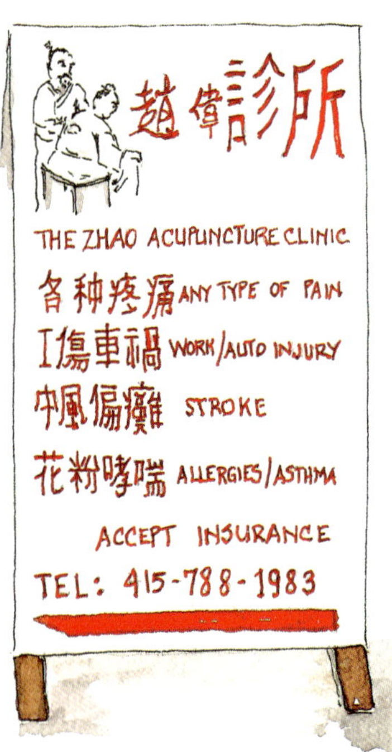

American Institute Of Nose Disease

中醫鼻病研究所

THE CHINESE HOSPITAL on Jackson Street in the heart of Chinatown offers both traditional Chinese as well as Western medicine. In fact, the neighborhood has many clinics to treat a wide variety of ailments.

food for sale at a typical Chinese market in Chinatown

THE PRESIDIO

1. Golden Gate Bridge
2. Fort Point
3. Crissy Field and beach
4. Pet Cemetery
5. Presidio Cemetery (San Francisco National Cemetery)
6. Montgomery Street Barracks
7. lagoon and shore birds
8. Funston Avenue houses
9. Officers' Club and Lovers' Lane

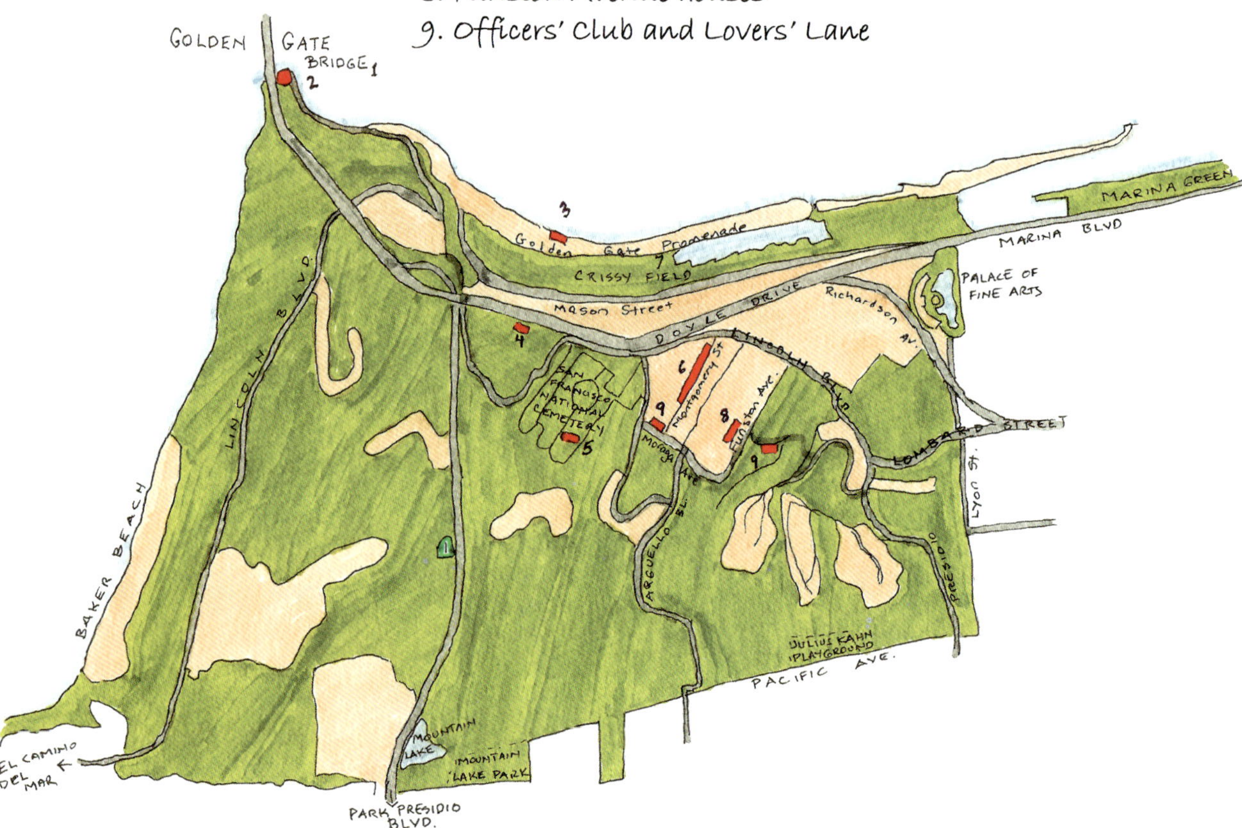

FORT POINT and the GOLDEN GATE BRIDGE

FORT POINT, a National Historic Site, was built at the height of the Civil War by the U.S. Army Corps of Engineers to protect San Francisco Bay from foreign attack and to keep the gold from the Confederate Army. The U.S. Army used it as barracks from the Civil War to the end of World War II, when soldiers from the Sixth U.S. Coast Guard Artillery were stationed here to guard minefields and the anti-submarine net that spanned the Golden Gate.

It has also been a popular film location. In one film, Alfred Hitchcock's *Vertigo*, Kim Novak's character, Madeleine, jumped into the bay in an apparent suicide attempt.

When the Golden Gate Bridge was under construction in the 1930s, there was talk of demolishing the fort, but fortunately, bridge engineer Joseph Strauss recognized its architectural and historical value and created a special engineering arch which allowed construction of the bridge to occur safely over the fort.

The art deco GOLDEN GATE BRIDGE was the longest single suspension bridge in the world when it was completed in 1937, but since then eight other bridges worldwide have outspanned it.

THE OFFICERS' CLUB above is one of the two oldest buildings in the city, (the other being Mission Dolores), though only part of the original adobe wall here built by the Spanish remains. In the 1930s it was remodeled into this graceful Spanish colonial revival style with rustic Spanish gable roofs, rough timber lintels and beams, and decorative ironwork.

LOVERS' LANE used to be the start of the road from the Presidio to Mission Dolores, three miles away. It meanders through Tennessee Hollow, starting at Funston Avenue and Presidio Boulevard, a lovely walk.

fog coming in through the Golden Gate in the early morning

The colonial style MONTGOMERY STREET BARRACKS, built between 1895 and 1897, housed troops during the Spanish-American War and occasionally after that for other conflicts overseas. It sits on Infantry Row along Crissy Field parade grounds, each of its buildings able to accommodate a company of 110 men and all with the same floor plan: ground floor with a recreation room, a mess hall and a kitchen; the upper two stories for sleeping. These brick barracks were constructed after the close of the frontier forts, the first in the western U.S., a demonstration of the Presidio's stature as a permanent and significant army post.

In 1995 the Presidio became a National Park when the Sixth Army left. The Walt Disney Family Foundation Museum moved into one of the barracks, and the International Center to End Violence will open in another. Other organizations and enterprises will fill in as the Presidio becomes financially self-sustaining.

a couple of shore birds in the lagoon

Civilians have been renting former Sixth Army housing, including this strip along Funston Avenue, since the Army left the Presidio in 1994 and it became part of the Golden Gate National Recreation Area.

Crissy Field Beach is a magnet on a beautiful day. Actually, on any given day, even a foggy one, walkers, dog walkers, bicyclists, joggers and surfing dudes who artfully dodge the rocks by Fort Point enjoy the fresh air and lovely views.

THE PRESIDIO CEMETERY

Soldiers from ten different wars are buried in this beautiful cemetery, one of only three remaining within the city limits (the other two are the Columbarium and Mission Dolores). Along with the soldiers there are two unusual burials: "Major" Pauline Cushman and Miss Sarah Bowman. Cushman's headstone reads "Pauline Fryer, Union spy." Bowman traveled with Zachary Taylor's troops in the Mexican War, helping to care for the wounded.

Author Kay Boyle and actor Percy Kilbride are also buried here.

IN MEMORY OF
JACK
BIK
CPL
US ARMY
WORLD WAR II
DEC 2 1922
FEB 24 1984

GEORGE J WILSON
PVT
US ARMY
SP.-AM WAR
JUL 4 1899

DAVID
ARTHUR
CLEMENTS
SP4
US ARMY
VIETNAM
NOV 2 1943
AUG 18 1972

JAMES C
McCARTY
CALIFORNIA
SGT
702 ORD MAINT.
2 INFANTRY DIV
KOREA
AUGUST 23 1930
OCTOBER 15 1959

DEAN H
REESER
CALIFORNIA
HORSESHOER
MED DEPT
WORLD WAR I
OCTOBER 18 1892
AUGUST 7 1968

MAJOR ELLERY W. EDDY
U.S. ARMY
JULY 30 1865

IN MEMORY OF
ABRAHAM
DESOMER
MEDAL OF HONOR
LCDR US NAVY
VERA CRUZ
MEXICO
DEC 29 1884
AUG 31 1934

ERECTED
BY
THE CREW OF THE
U.S.S. OREGON
IN MEMORY OF
THEIR SHIPMATES PRIVATES
HARRY FISHER,
ALBERT TURNER,
ROBERT E. THOMAS,
CHARLES B. KING,
U.S. MARINE CORPS,
KILLED IN ACTION ON THE
TARTAR WALL
OF
PEKING CHINA
IN DEFENSE OF THE
LEGATIONS
DURING THE
BOXER HOSTILITIES
OF THE SUMMER OF
1900

First Lieutenant
ARTHUR CRANSTON,
Fourth Regiment
of U.S. Artillery.
Killed in action with
Modoc Indians
in the Lava Beds
California
April 26, 1873
"Greater love hath no man
than this, that a man lay
down his life for his friend"

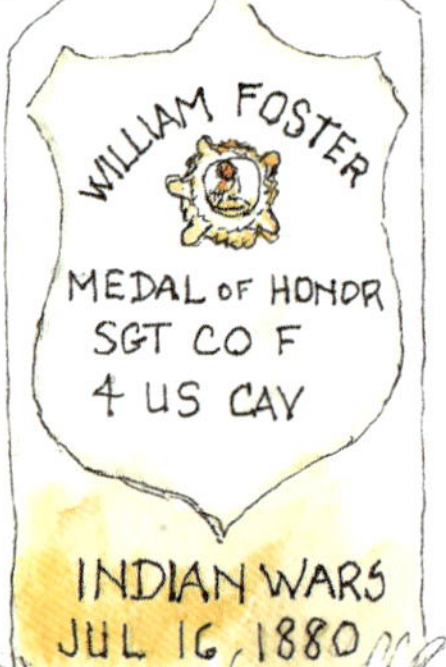

The Presidio Pet Cemetery, one of the most charming spots in the city, was in danger of demolition as the widening of Doyle Drive began, but neighbors and the gods intervened to stop it.

NORTHWEST SAN FRANCISCO

(minus The Presidio)

中國海灘

CHINA BEACH

SINCE GOLD RUSH TIMES, THIS COVE WAS USED AS A CAMPSITE BY MANY OF THE CHINESE FISHERMEN WHO WORKED IN AND AROUND SAN FRANCISCO BAY. THEIR EFFORTS TO SUPPLY THE NEEDS OF A YOUNG CITY HELPED ESTABLISH ONE OF THE AREA'S MOST IMPORTANT INDUSTRIES AND TRADITIONS.

GIFT OF HENRY & DIANA CHUNG FAMILY 1981

1. Octagon House
2. Filbert Street row
3. St. Mary the Virgin courtyard
4. Chestnut Street
5. Palace of Fine Arts
6. Wave Organ
7. Victorian on California & Octavia
8. Haas-Lilienthal House
9. Webster Street row
10. China Beach
11. Cottage Row
12. a Maybeck house
13. a Wurster house & roof
14. Jackson & Cherry Street house
15. Temple Emanu-el
16. St. John's Presbyterian Church
17. Swedenborgian Church
18. houses along Presidio wall
19. Clement Street restaurants
20. The Green Apple
21. Mountain Lake Park
22. Lake Street house
23. Holy Virgin Cathedral
24. California Street cottages
25. Little Russia
26. Holocaust Memorial
27. Legion of Honor
28. Cliff House
29. Ocean Beach
30. Seal Rocks

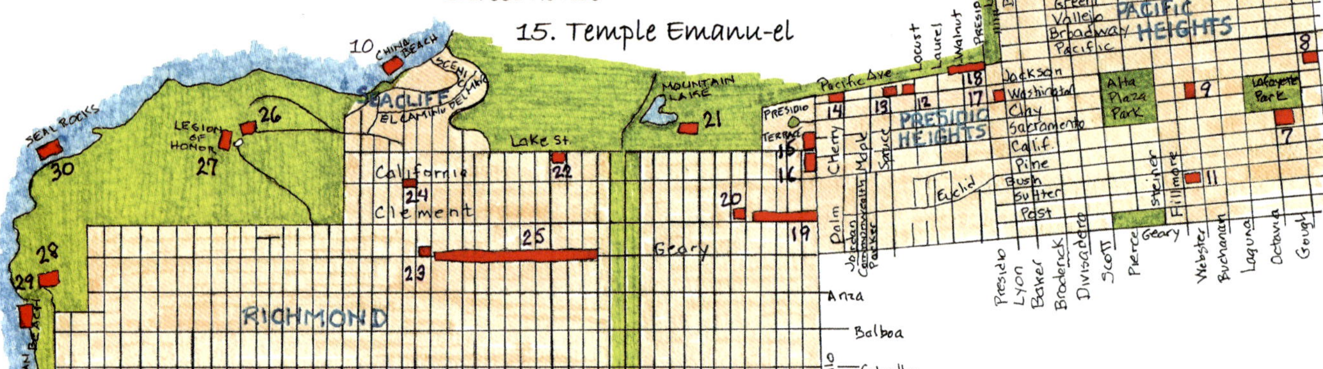

COW HOLLOW

Located between the Marina and Pacific Heights, Cow Hollow is tony and attractive. On the right is a Queen Anne Victorian, and below is one of San Francisco's two remaining octagon houses, located on Gough between Union and Green.

Octagon houses were all built during a temporary craze for eight-sided houses, this one in 1861. Maximum exposure to light was thought to promote good health. This one offers tours three times a month. The other remaining octagon house is privately owned, on Russian Hill.

On the right is part of a mural in the courtyard of St. Mary the Virgin Episcopal Church on the corner of Steiner and Union Streets.

a row of houses on Filbert Street

CHESTNUT STREET

Kara's Cupcakes - yum!

lunch on a sunny day with a glass of wine or a Diet Coke

Fireside: my favorite camera shop in the whole world...

THE DOGS OF
CHESTNUT
STREET
SALE
dog at the deli
Bud at the
Apple store

THE MARINA

THE PALACE OF FINE ARTS was built for the Panama Pacific International Exposition in 1915, designed by Bernard Maybeck, who was inspired by Greek and Roman architecture.

THE WAVE ORGAN is an acoustic sculpture set into a little peninsula that juts into the bay across from the Marina Green. A work of environmental art, it is best at high tide. The sounds that come through are rumbles, gurgles, hisses, sloshes and other typical wave sounds.

PACIFIC HEIGHTS VICTORIANS

a row of Italianates on Webster just off Washington

A PAIR OF QUEEN ANNES

On the left is an elaborate Queen Anne on California and Octavia. The Haas-Lilienthal house, above right, was built in 1886 and still has its original furnishings.

COTTAGE ROW and the WEBSTER STREET HISTORIC DISTRICT

The six cottages of COttage Row sit on a brick walkway between Sutter and Bush, and Webster and Fillmore, each a twenty-foot lot. In the 1930s the Japanese-Americans who lived in them grew vegetables in their tiny back gardens and sold them in an open market every Saturday. In those days the row was Called Japan Street. But in one of the most tragic episodes in our history, our government interned the residents, along with 110,000 other Japanese-Americans, and they never returned to these cottages. After the war, new owners moved in.

The house on the right is on Bush, just off Webster, and is also part of the Webster Street Historic District.

Zippy is the Cottage Row mascot

PACIFIC and PRESIDIO HEIGHTS: TWO CHURCHES and a SYNAGOGUE

The Swedenborgian Church, on the National Register of Historic Places, is a fine example of the early Arts & Crafts movement. A group that included William Worcester, its first pastor, and Bernard Maybeck founded it in 1895.

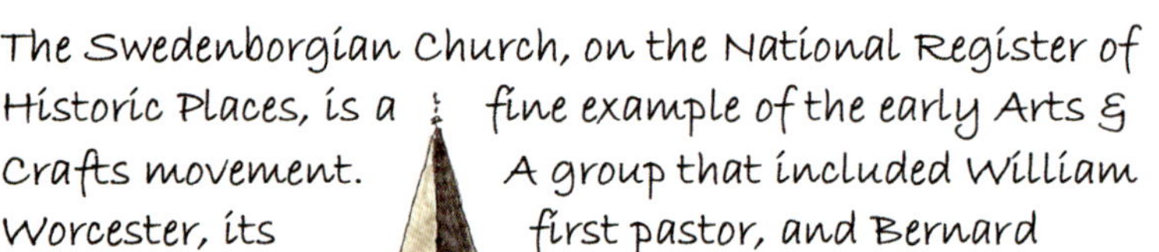

The Swedenborgian Church on Lyon off Washington

St. John's Presbyterian Church on Arguello and Lake

Temple Emanu-el on Arguello and Lake

Also on the National Register, St. John's came to Lake & Arguello in 1906, suffered heavy damage in the earthquake and was rebuilt in 1907.

The Hagia Sophia in Istanbul inspired the design of Temple Emanu-el, dedicated in 1926. The original congregation was founded in 1850.

FOUR PRESIDIO HEIGHTS HOMES

Coxhead-designed houses sitting along the Presidio wall on Pacific Avenue.

below: mansion on Jackson & Cherry

Top right: a Maybeck-designed house at 3500 Jackson at Laurel
Above right: The William Wurster-designed Sutro house on Jackson & Spruce has a lovely Mansard roof and a New Orleans-style front courtyard.

LAKE STREET

Lake Street is a village unto itself: colorful houses, tree-lined streets, lots of children and lovely Mountain Lake Park almost hidden behind the houses from 7th to 12th Avenues.

Bird Beach - Mountain Lake

cottages on
California Street between
27th and 28th Avenues

THE RICHMOND

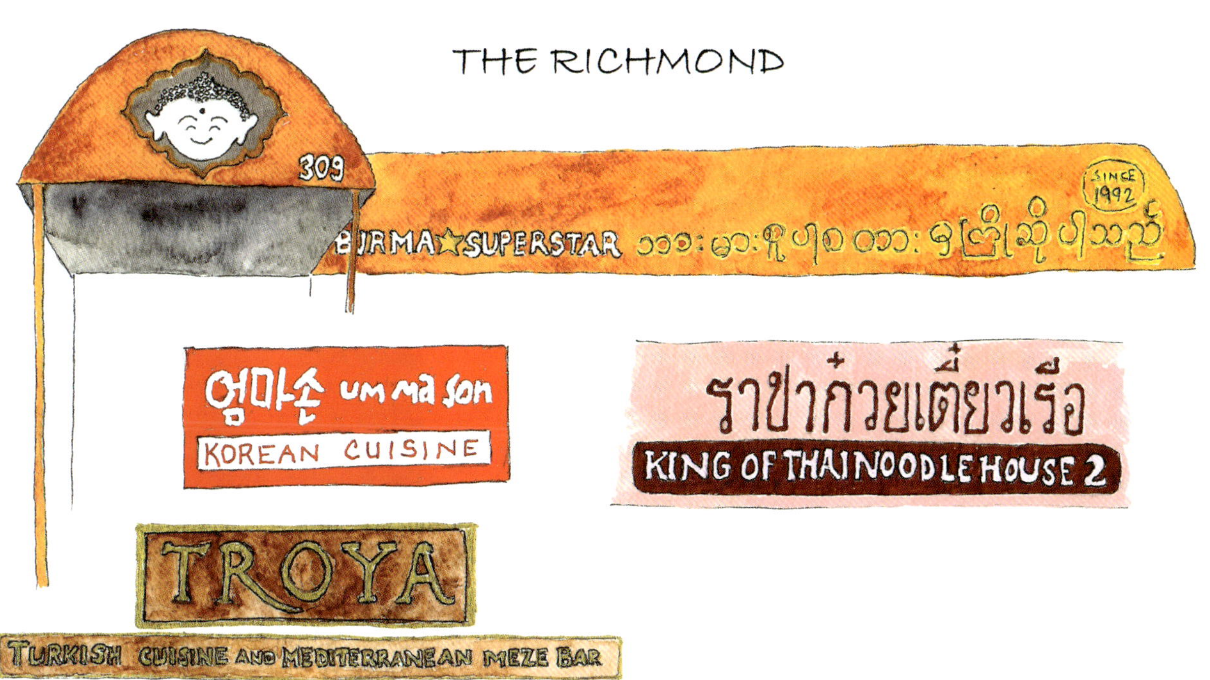

What an ethnic variety of restaurants there is on Clement Street between Arguello and Sixth Avenue... Burma Superstar, for example, at 307 Clement is a neighborhood gem, worth the notoriously long waits for tasty items like Tangy Tea Leaf Salad and Spicy Samusa Soup.

THE GREEN APPLE

For many years I've been taking some of my used books to The Green Apple, which sells both new and used books, music, videos, audio books, cd's and magazines.

fall colors in San Francisco

ЕЛИСЕЕВСКИЙ
ДЕЛИКАТЕСЫ
RUSSIAN-EUROPIAN DELI CATERING DELIVERY
РУССКОЕ ВИДЕО

LITTLE RUSSIA

wind-blown cypress trees on Land's End

In much of the Outer Richmond, you'd think you were in Moscow. In fact, the Russians have been here a while. A Russian nobleman came in 1806 and promptly fell in love with the daughter of the Spanish governor. In the 1950s, the city became home to a number of Russian émigrés who had fled the Revolution, first to China and Europe and then after World War II to San Francisco. Holy Trinity Cathedral, built in the 1960s, is crowned with five gold-leafed onion domes and includes mosaics, frescoes, icons and relics of Orthodox saints. It is one of several Russian Orthodox churches in San Francisco.

SEA CLIFF

Outside the Legion of Honor, near the reflecting pool, is George Segal's solemn Holocaust Memorial sculpture.

Sea Cliff is a neighborhood of expensive homes, mostly on large lots, many perched on the cliffs that overlook the strait between SF and Marin and the Golden Gate Bridge. Streets wind around each other, and residents don't seem to mind the fog that hovers just about all summer long.

The LEGION OF HONOR, opened in 1924, was a gift to the city from Adolph and Alma Spreckels. The museum commemorates servicemen who died in World War I. It is French neo-classical in style, an exact three-quarters replica of the Palais de la Legion d'Honneur in Paris, where Napoleon Bonaparte paid tribute to his soldiers. The colonnated courtyard marks the entrance to the museum and a backdrop for an original casting of Rodin's *The Thinker.*

Seal Rocks and a couple of their visitors

Ocean Beach on a stormy day

The Cliff House sits on a rocky point looking out at Seal Rocks. It is not the original Cliff House - that one burned down. If you want to eat with a view, this is a great place to do it.

- THE END -

INDEX

<u>COMMERCIAL</u>

SKETCHING SAN FRANCISCO'S NEIGHBORHOODS
Eleanor Burke

Publisher: Nguyen Thi Thanh Huong
Editor: Hong Duc
Proof Reader: Thanh Van

Ho Chi Minh City General Publishing House
General Bookstore
62 Nguyen Thi Minh Khai, Dist. 1, HCMC

Quantity: 3000 copies, size 21cm x 21cm
Printed in Vietnam, at Tran Phu Printing Company,
71-75 Hai Ba Trung St., Dist. 1, HCMC
Publication Permit No. 828-11/CXB/18-68/THTPHCM 08/08/2011
Sent to archives: August, 2011

ISBN number: 978-0-615-42402-6
First printing Jan 2011
Second printing Aug 2011

Orders, inquiries and correspondence: Eleanor Burke (415) 567-4944, egburke@earthlink.net